Hashtag Hustle

Your Guide to Social Media Wealth

By
William Frye

Copyright 2023 The Mattress Maverick. All rights reserved.

No part of this book may be reproduced in any form or by any electronic or mechanical means including information storage and retrieval systems, without permission in writing from the author. The only exception is by a reviewer, who may quote short excerpts in a review.

Although the author and publisher have made every effort to ensure that the information in this book was correct at press time, the author and publisher do not assume and hereby disclaim any liability to any party for any loss, damage, or disruption caused by errors or omissions, whether such errors or omissions result from negligence, accident, or any other cause.

This publication is designed to provide accurate and authoritative information with regard to the subject matter covered. It is sold with the understanding that the publisher is not engaged in rendering professional services. If legal advice or other expert assistance is required, the services of a competent professional should be sought.

The fact that an organization or website is referred to in this work as a citation and/or a potential source of further information does not mean that the author or the publisher endorses the information the organization or website may provide or recommendations it may make.

Please remember that Internet websites listed in this work may have changed or disappeared between when this work was written and when it is read.

Hashtag Hustle

Your Guide to Social Media Wealth

Contents

Introduction 1
   Embracing the Digital Hustle: The Power of Social Media 3

Chapter 1: The Fundamentals of Social Media Wealth 6
   Your Social Media Wealth Journey 6
   Platforms that Pay: Where to Focus Your Energy 7
   Your Social Media Wealth Journey 8
   Platforms that Pay: Where to Focus Your Energy 11

Chapter 2: Building a Money-Making Facebook Empire 14
   Crafting a Compelling Facebook Presence 14
   Monetizing Your Facebook Audience 15
   Crafting a Compelling Facebook Presence 16
   Monetizing Your Facebook Audience 18
   From Likes to Loot: Strategies for Profit 20

Chapter 3: Instagram Cash Flows:
Capturing the Visual Market 24
   The Aesthetics of Income: Your Instagram Blueprint 24
   Converting Followers Into Dollars 25
   Influencer Secrets: Partnerships and Sponsorships 25
   The Aesthetics of Income: Your Instagram Blueprint 26
   Converting Followers Into Dollars 29
   Understand Your Audience 29
   Provide Genuine Value 30
   Engage With Purpose 30
   Exclusive Offers 30
   Track and Adapt 31

Influencer Secrets: Partnerships and Sponsorships 31

Chapter 4: Mastering Threads: The Untapped Goldmine 35
Understanding Threads and Its Earning Potential...................... 35
Navigating the Do's and Don'ts of Threads Engagement 36
Understanding Threads and Its Earning Potential...................... 37
Navigating the Do's and Don'ts of Threads Engagement 40

Chapter 5: The TikTok Takeover: Short Videos, Big Bucks 43
TikTok Basics for Viral Success 43
Monetizing Trends: Beyond Dancing Clips............................. 43
The Algorithm Advantage: Timing and Hashtags...................... 44
TikTok Basics for Viral Success 45
Monetizing Trends: Beyond Dancing Clips............................. 47
The Algorithm Advantage: Timing and Hashtags...................... 49

Chapter 6: Going Viral: Your Blueprint for
Social Media Fame...53
The Virality Factor: What Makes Content Spread 53
Leveraging Viral Content for Maximum Earnings 54
The Virality Factor: What Makes Content Spread 54
Leveraging Viral Content for Maximum Earnings 57

Chapter 7: Lights, Camera, Cash: Crafting
Perfect Video Clips...61
Video Content that Sells: Quality and Engagement 61
Tools of the Trade: Must-Have Gadgets and Software 62
Video Content that Sells: Quality and Engagement 62
Tools of the Trade: Must-Have Gadgets and Software 65

Chapter 8: Do-It-Yourself or Outsource?
The Solo Hustler's Dilemma 69
Pros and Cons of Independent Content Creation....................... 70
When to Consider Outsourcing... 73
Finding and Managing Freelancers 75

v

**Chapter 9: Work Smarter, Not Harder:
Automation and Tools** **79**
   Essential Social Media Tools for Efficiency 79
   Automating Your Way to Passive Income 80
   Essential Social Media Tools for Efficiency 81
   Automating Your Way to Passive Income 83

Chapter 10: Building Your Social Media Brand **87**
   Defining Your Online Persona 87
   Trust and Authenticity: The Currencies of Social Media 88
   Defining Your Online Persona 89
   Trust and Authenticity: The Currencies of Social Media 92

Chapter 11: The Legal Side of Social Media Earnings **95**
   Understanding Copyrights, Sponsorships and Disclosures 95
   Protecting Yourself and Your Profits Online 95
   Understanding Copyrights, Sponsorships and Disclosures 96
   Protecting Yourself and Your Profits Online 99

**Chapter 12: Beyond the Platforms:
Diversifying Your Online Income** **103**
   Creating Your Own Products and Courses 103
   Exploring Membership Sites and Patreon 104
   Creating Your Own Products and Courses 104
   Exploring Membership Sites and Patreon 107

Conclusion **111**
   Sustaining Your Social Media Success 111
   Sustaining Your Social Media Success 112

Appendix A: Appendix **115**
   Resource Directory: Tools, Platforms, and Services 115
   Resource Directory: Tools, Platforms, and Services 116

Glossary of Social Media Terms **120**
   Algorithm 120

Analytics 120
Brand Ambassador 120
Content Calendar 120
Engagement Rate 121
Followers 121
Hashtag 121
Influencer 121
Monetization 121
Sponsored Post 122
Stories 122
User-Generated Content (UGC) 122
Frequently Asked Questions: Quick Answers to Common
Concerns 122
Frequently Asked Questions: Quick Answers to Common
Concerns 122

Introduction

Imagine turning the device in your pocket or the laptop in your home into a digital goldmine. Envision harnessing the connective power of social media not just to share moments or ideas, but to create a substantial stream of income right from the comfort of your home. With the digital landscape expanding at an unprecedented rate, the opportunity to make money online through platforms like TikTok, Facebook, Instagram, and emerging channels such as Threads is not only possible, it's becoming the new norm for savvy digital entrepreneurs.

In this resource, you'll embark on a journey through the bustling world of social media monetization. We're breaking down the walls of mystery around the digital hustle and transforming your understanding of what it means to make money in today's interconnected world. Expanding beyond traditional job paradigms, this book offers a roadmap to financial freedom and empowerment through platforms that are already part of your daily routine.

As you flip through the pages, you will uncover the secrets to building a wealth-generating empire, one post at a time. We're not talking about get-rich-quick schemes; instead, we focus on proven strategies that leverage the innate power of social engagement and creative content to establish a sustainable income.

This journey won't just be about learning the mechanisms of various platforms. You'll delve into the heart of what makes content click, understand the dynamics of audience retention, decode the algorithms, and most importantly, learn how to consistently convert your efforts into earnings. It's about finding your niche, crystallizing your message, and reaching out to an audience eager to consume what you have to offer.

Whether you're drawn to the visual appeal of Instagram, the community strength of Facebook, the dynamic short-form world of TikTok, or you're curious about how to pioneer the newer channels, we have you covered. With every chapter, you'll gain insights on utilizing each platform to its fullest potential so that you can not only grow your online presence but also your bank account.

Let this be your inspirational guide and instructional handbook in one, a beacon to light the path to success on your terms. Stand on the edge of possibility, ready to take control of your financial future, and let's transform your passion for social media into profits. Welcome to your digital revolution; let's make it count.

William Frye Sr. AKA: The Mattress Maverick spends an average of 6-8 months traveling for a variety of reasons. Mostly for pleasure, fishing, eating, taking nature pictures, writing for his next book/adventure, etc.... So, to label myself as a self proclaimed travelling foodie, isn't a far stretch. I love to eat, and I love good eating even more. So, if you happen to see me out and about the globe somewhere, feel free to say HI. Maybe we can even share a meal together wherever we happen to be. Do I pack up the RV, camper or other recreational vehicle to do my travelling? Nope, I do not. I personally pack up my car and get on the road or in some cases the ocean. This lifestyle is custom made for the online sales world. Are you ready to travel, make money in your spare time from your laptop while sitting on a beach somewhere while sipping on one of those "umbrella drinks"? Well, put the tools that you'll find inside these pages to work, and you'll be free to enjoy whatever it is you choose to enjoy soon enough. It's time to live live, Happy & Safe travels, and may you find favor in all that you set out to do.

Embracing the Digital Hustle: The Power of Social Media

The realm of social media is much more than a space for sharing selfies and keeping up with friends. It's a vibrant ecosystem where entrepreneurship thrives and where your presence could potentially translate into profit. Embracing the digital hustle means recognizing the transformative power of social media platforms to turn creativity and influence into revenue streams. Whether you're a seasoned veteran or a fresh face online, understanding this can set the foundation for your financial success.

Every swipe, like, and follow on platforms like TikTok, Facebook, and Instagram presents an opportunity. Each allows you to reach across the digital expanse, connecting you to a global audience eager to consume, engage, and invest in the brand that you build – your personal brand. It's time we pivot our perspective on social media usage from passive scrolling to active engagement and content creation that pays off.

The influence economy is booming, and it's rooted in the currency of attention. Your capacity to captivate and hold the attention of others is invaluable. When you strike the right chord with an audience, you become more than just another user – you become an asset that businesses and brands are willing to invest in. Partnering with companies, leveraging affiliate links, and even selling your own merchandise are just a few avenues to explore.

Within the scope of this digital revolution, content is king, but consistency is the key to the kingdom. Consistency in message, brand, and engagement forms the cornerstone of trust with your following. And in the world of social media, trust translates into influence, and influence equates to opportunities for monetization. Every post, every story, every live broadcast can become a conduit through which you can funnel your entrepreneurial aspirations into reality.

Technology has broken down the barriers that once relegated business to the confines of brick-and-mortar establishments. Your cellphone or laptop is now your storefront, your office, and your marketing department all in one. This portability of business means you can operate from anywhere at any time, making it a perfect venture for anyone looking to monetize their digital presence from the comfort of their home.

Understanding current trends and algorithmic nuances is vital to turn your social media activity into a revenue-generating enterprise. The TikTok takeover, for instance, isn't just about short, catchy videos – it's a study in viral content creation and strategic hashtag use to harness the platform's algorithm. Similarly, Instagram's visual marketplace isn't just about pretty pictures; it's about building a narrative that sells – a story that your audience can buy into.

But where exactly should you focus your energy? The landscape is vast, and resources, though abundant, are finite. This section won't delve deep into the specifics of each platform – that's reserved for the coming chapters. Instead, it's about preparing you to engage with social media not just as a user, but as a digital entrepreneur, laying the groundwork for the targeted tactics to be outlined later on.

Let's also consider the transformative potential of threads and other emerging platforms that might not have hit mainstream status yet but are ripe with opportunity for early adopters. Recognizing these platforms can offer you a first-mover advantage, positioning you to capitalize on growth and monetization opportunities before they become oversaturated.

Social media has also democratized fame. Virality can turn the average person into an overnight sensation. This rapid change of fortune isn't just serendipity; it's a craft that involves understanding the psychology of sharing and the mechanics of content distribution. Mastering this isn't a stroke of luck – it's a skill you can cultivate.

Amidst all this strategic maneuvering, an essential aspect to bear in mind is authenticity. The most impactful online personas are those that are firmly rooted in genuineness and relatability. Your audience isn't just looking for content; they are looking for a connection. Being yourself, transparently and unapologetically, can be your greatest asset in the digital arena.

With each chapter ahead, we'll dive into strategies, tips, and tricks to turn those 'double taps', views, and comments into a viable income. From learning how to craft compelling Facebook posts that resonate with your audience to exploiting Instagram's aesthetic pull, you'll gain insight into the varied paths towards achieving social media wealth.

But remember, success on social media isn't just about what you post; it's also about how you engage. The strength of your digital brand is proportional to the strength of the community you build around it. Engagement doesn't stop with your content; it's about fostering interactions and nurturing the relationships that you form online.

Before we proceed, let's take a moment to reflect on your aspirations. Aligning these with the potential that social media holds is paramount. What are your passions? What value can you offer? How can you differentiate yourself in a crowded market? The answers to these questions are the compass by which you'll navigate the vast seas of online opportunities.

Through these pages, let the notion of the digital hustle empower you. Approach social media with the mindset of someone ready to claim their slice of the digital pie – and be hungry to learn and adapt. Social media isn't static; it's continually evolving. Staying abreast with its changing facets is what will keep your online hustle thriving. You now stand at the precipice of something great, armed with knowledge and on the cusp of opportunity. Let's transform your vision into reality.

Chapter 1:
The Fundamentals of Social Media Wealth

Welcome to the beginning of your transformative journey through the terrain of social media wealth. In this first chapter, we're diving into the foundational strategies and principles you need to understand before you can navigate the social media landscape to accrue wealth. It's about more than just posting selfies or tweeting your thoughts; it's about leveraging a variety of platforms to create a sustainable, profitable online presence that can translate into real-world earnings.

Let's start with a universal truth: social media has changed the way the world communicates, connects, and, crucially, conducts business. Today, with a smart strategy and a knack for engagement, anyone can turn their online platform into a source of income. But how does one go from casual user to social media maven? It begins with understanding where to direct your energy.

Your Social Media Wealth Journey

Embarking on your social media wealth journey involves more than just choosing the right platforms—it's about adopting the mindset of a digital entrepreneur. Your approach must be both flexible and focused, always ready to learn and pivot, but dedicated to your chosen paths. The wealth journey is one of continuous growth, network building, and strategic planning, propelled by an entrepreneurial spirit that seeks opportunity in every post and interaction. Success in this space is a testament to persistence, creativity, and adaptability.

Platforms that Pay: Where to Focus Your Energy

While there are myriad platforms at your disposal, not all are created equal when it comes to monetization potentials. To create wealth, you need to know which platforms offer the best return on your time and effort investments. Facebook, Instagram, TikTok, and the emerging platform Threads, among others, each offer unique avenues for generating income.

However, it's not just about being present on these platforms; it's about understanding the mechanics of each. Who are the users? What content performs best? And how does the platform reward its content creators? To carve out a profitable niche, you'll need to align your content with the interests and behaviors of the platform's user base.

This chapter has laid the groundwork for your social media wealth journey, offering a taste of the potential that awaits. As you progress through subsequent chapters, you'll dive deeper into specific platforms and strategies. You'll learn how to build up a dominant Facebook presence, captivate audiences on Instagram, master the intricacies of Threads, and utilize TikTok for significant earnings.

Remember, within the digital hustle lies the power to craft a narrative that resonates, build a community that engages, and create content that not only captivates but also converts. As you move ahead, keep in mind that each platform is a new realm to conquer, each post a step closer to your goals, and each follower a potential key to unlocking the wealth that awaits.

Your success story in the lucrative world of social media is just waiting to be written. Let this journey illuminate your path and inspire your spirit. The time is now; the opportunity is yours—seize it.

Your Social Media Wealth Journey

The landscape of making money has been revolutionized by the age of social media, offering an incredible opportunity to generate wealth right from the comfort of your home. This journey is not only about understanding the tools of the trade but also about mapping out a strategic pathway that is driven by your passions, creativity, and the unique value you can offer.

Embarking on your social media wealth journey, you'll find that the digital sphere is bursting with potential. Whether you're scrolling through TikTok, Facebook, Instagram, or exploring emerging platforms like Threads, each medium offers unique avenues to capitalize on your online presence. It's about harnessing the power of content creation, community building, and strategic marketing to convert likes, shares, and follows into a sustainable income.

The first step on this exciting path is self-assessment. Question what you're truly passionate about and how that intersects with what is marketable. Identifying this sweet spot is crucial. It's the convergence of passion and demand that will sustain your motivation and attract an audience that is genuinely interested in what you have to say or sell.

Once you've pinpointed your niche, it's time to dive deep into content creation. One of the most compelling attributes of social media is its hunger for fresh content. Viewers are always on the lookout for new, engaging, and transformative content — the kind that enriches their lives or provides them with a much-needed laugh. Creating content that resonates with your audience, while remaining genuine and authentic to your voice, will be a continuous process throughout your journey.

Understanding the individual ecosystems of each platform is also part of the voyage. Facebook's landscape is vastly different from Instagram's, and TikTok operates on yet another wavelength. Each platform will require specific strategies for engagement and monetization, which you will master over time. Learning the nuances, such as when to post and what kind of content performs well, will help you tailor your social media strategy to each platform effectively.

Building a following is a marathon, not a sprint. It's a commitment to consistent and quality engagement with your audience. Social media wealth isn't achieved overnight; rather, it's cultivated through daily interactions, listening to feedback, and adapting to the ebbs and flows of online trends. Your community is your stronghold, and fostering those relationships is equivalent to nurturing your revenue stream.

As you grow, monetization strategies will become more apparent. Perhaps you'll leverage Facebook's marketplace, dive into Instagram's shopping features, or utilize TikTok's creator fund. You might even partner with brands for sponsorships or create your own digital products. Each option represents a step along the path to financial freedom and forms part of a diversified income strategy that you'll learn to grasp and optimize.

Let's not overlook the importance of analytics and the insights they provide. Monitoring what works and what doesn't allows you to make informed decisions that propel your social media wealth journey forward. Optimization is the key to growth and scaling your online presence, which, in turn, scales your earnings.

Throughout this journey, remember that adaptability is your greatest ally. The social media landscape is always shifting, with new platforms rising to fame and algorithms continually updating. Staying ahead of the curve requires you to be flexible, ready to pivot your strategies, and embrace new technologies or platforms that may enhance your online endeavors.

Equally significant is the reality of setbacks and challenges. Hurdles are an inherent part of any venture, and your social media journey will be no different. Each obstacle is an opportunity to learn, refine, and overcome — strengthening your resolve and expertise in the process.

As you gain momentum, don't hesitate to invest in yourself. Whether it's in the form of educational resources, premium tools, or outsourcing to talented freelancers, investing in your growth is fundamental to escalating your social media venture. Remember, it's always about working smarter, not just harder.

Alongside the practical steps, never underestimate the power of mindset. Maintaining a positive, growth-oriented psyche will empower you to surpass the expectations of others, and more importantly, the limits you've previously set for yourself. Celebrate your victories, learn from your losses, and keep pushing the boundaries of what's possible.

Your social media wealth journey is unique to you. There's no one-size-fits-all blueprint to success. It's a personalized tapestry woven with threads of your individual experiences, insights, and creative flair. Embrace your individuality and let it shine through every post, video, and interaction.

Finally, connect with like-minded individuals. The value of a network cannot be overemphasized in the social media realm. Sharing ideas, collaborating, and supporting each other can catalyze growth in ways you might not achieve solo. As you build your wealth, remember the shared journey with peers can be just as rewarding as the financial gains.

So, gear up for an exhilarating odyssey. Your social media wealth journey isn't just about building an income; it's about creating a life enriched by meaningful connections, creative freedom, and the joy of making your mark in the digital world. Keep learning, keep evolving, and watch as your efforts translate into a tangible, thriving online empire.

Platforms that Pay: Where to Focus Your Energy

Diving into the vast sea of social media can feel overwhelming, with every platform offering its own quirks and potential for profit. However, not all platforms are created equal when it comes to monetizing your presence. But where should you maximize your efforts to transform likes into a livable wage? Let's break it down, platform by platform, without going too far into the weeds on any one — as we'll elaborate on these further in their respective chapters.

First off, let's talk about Facebook. It's a juggernaut. With over 2 billion active users, the opportunities are immense. It's a marketplace, it's a community builder, it's a news source, and for you, it can also be a gold mine. If you're looking to sell products, market services, or simply build brand recognition, Facebook's diverse tools and broad audience make it a go-to platform.

Instagram, on the other hand, is the king of visual content. If you're looking to captivate an audience with stunning images or stories, then harnessing the power of Instagram is a must. It's perfect for lifestyle, fashion, and beauty influencers, as well as photographers and artists. Moreover, with features like Instagram Shopping and IGTV, there are numerous ways to direct your followers towards monetization channels.

Don't overlook Threads. Being the new kid on the block, it offers uncharted territory ripe with opportunity. As we will delve into in Chapter 4, Threads is particularly appealing for those who excel at crafting more intimate and engaged communities.

Then there's the TikTok phenomenon. This platform has reshaped what it means to go viral. Unlike others, TikTok's algorithm provides an unparalleled opportunity for your content to be seen by millions, regardless of how many followers you have. Learn its rhythms and you can ride its waves all the way to the bank.

Now, every platform has its nuances, and success requires understanding these details. For instance, video content is becoming increasingly important across all networks — not just TikTok. Platforms like YouTube and even LinkedIn are rewarding creators who can produce engaging and shareable video content.

Let's not forget about Twitter, where the currency is information and wit, it's an excellent venue for establishing yourself as a thought leader or brand voice and for jumping into trending conversations that could get your name out there.

For those with a knack for crafting compelling written content, Medium could be your sweet spot. It's a platform allowing deep dives into nearly any topic under the sun, and if you can forge a strong connection with readers, Medium's Partner Program can be a consistent revenue stream.

When evaluating where to focus your energy, it's also essential to consider your strengths and what type of content creation excites you. Are you a natural in front of the camera? Then YouTube, TikTok, and Instagram might be your best bets. Do you write like a dream? Blogs, Facebook, and Twitter can be your playground.

It's not just about choosing one platform, either. The most successful social media entrepreneurs often cast a wide net but identify where their primary audience resides. Cross-promoting content can help you capture followers from various platforms and guide them to where you're most active.

And remember, while chasing the latest trends can be lucrative, longevity in this space often boils down to authenticity. Build genuine relationships with your followers wherever you are, and they'll follow you, quite literally, to the ends of the earth — or at least across their favorite social media platforms.

With that foundation, it's crucial to have a pulse on which platforms are on an upward trajectory. This savvy insight will allow you to be an early adopter of emerging networks, setting you up as a leading figure before the competition becomes too stiff.

To truly harness the power of social media, consistency is your ally. Each post, video, or tweet is a brick in the empire you're building. So wherever you choose to focus that energy, make sure you're ready to commit. The combination of a consistent message with a consistent schedule is the not-so-secret sauce to longevity and profitability.

Finally, don't get too comfortable. The digital landscape is famously fickle. Stay adaptable, keep learning, and be ready to pivot when platforms evolve or new ones arise. By keeping your finger on the pulse of digital trends, you'll stay ahead of the curve and avoid losing relevance.

In the end, where you focus your energy will depend on where your talents shine brightest and where your audience lives. Consider your content, your audience, and your personal brand when choosing your platforms. Align these correctly, and you'll unlock the formula to a sustainable and profitable social media presence.

The next chapters will peel back the layers of how to succeed on individual platforms, but for now, understand this: your success is not about spreading yourself thin across every network. It's about intensifying your efforts where they count the most. Find your niche, dominate your platform, and watch as your social media efforts convert into a steady stream of wealth. That's what we're here to achieve.

Chapter 2:
Building a Money-Making Facebook Empire

Having planted your feet firmly in the fertile soil of social media wealth, it's time now to cultivate your digital landscape, beginning with the behemoth that is Facebook. The platform's sprawling user base is not just an audience, it's a diverse marketplace full of opportunities for those ready to tap into its potential.

Achieving financial success through Facebook isn't just about posting content; it requires strategic planning, brand development, and engagement skills that convert connections into income. As we dive into this chapter, you'll discover how to create a Facebook presence that resonates with your target audience and, critically, how to turn that resonance into revenue.

Crafting a Compelling Facebook Presence

The first cornerstone for building your empire is to forge a compelling online persona. Your Facebook profile and pages are your digital storefronts, mirrors reflecting the brand you wish to champion. Photography, biography, and even the tone of your posts should all align to tell the cohesive story of your brand. Authenticity is key; users are drawn to engaging, relatable content that speaks to their interests and needs.

Your content strategy must be robust and versatile, leveraging the various formats Facebook encourages. Embrace everything from text posts that start conversations to live videos that bring your audience behind the scenes of your daily life or business operations. Each piece of content is a brick in the empire you're building, so make sure each one is laid with intent and purpose.

Monetizing Your Facebook Audience

With a compelling presence comes the capacity to monetize. Understanding your audience—their demographics, their desires, their digital behavior—is critical to transforming your Facebook following into a revenue stream. Whether it's through targeted advertising, creating monetizable content, or hosting paid online events, each avenue opens up new ways to turn likes and shares into a measurable income.

The recipe for a money-making Facebook empire contains various ingredients—affiliate marketing, sponsored content, and even selling your products or services directly through the platform. Diversify your approach, test different monetization strategies, and see which ones resonate most with your audience. It's not just about selling; it's about providing value in a way that aligns with your brand story and your followers' expectations.

Every empire takes time to build, and the same holds true for your presence on Facebook. Patience, coupled with consistent effort and strategy, will guide you in transforming your social media endeavors into a source of income. Focus on engaging your audience, understand the metrics that matter, and always, always be adapting—because in the realm of social media, change is the only constant.

Remember, this is just the beginning. With the foundation we lay here, you'll be primed to extend your influence to other social media platforms. But for now, concentrate on the tasks at hand—nurturing your Facebook community, crafting content that captivates, and deploying monetization strategies that convert. Let's turn your digital empire into a reality, one post at a time.

Crafting a Compelling Facebook Presence

Crafting a compelling Facebook presence is about more than just a profile picture and a bio. It's about creating a digital persona that captivates and engages your audience—turning followers into fans, and fans into customers. By honing a distinctive online presence, you are laying the cornerstone for a money-making Facebook empire.

The initial step is clear: you need to identify your niche. A well-defined niche helps you target content and build a dedicated audience who genuinely resonates with what you offer. Consistency is key here. Whether you're a whiz in the kitchen, a fitness addict, or a tech guru, your content must reflect your niche in every post, photo, and comment.

Your profile itself must also tell a compelling story. This means a professional and pertinent profile picture, and a cover photo that encapsulates the essence of your brand. Your 'About' section should be succinct yet informative, outlining who you are, what you do, and why people should care.

Content creation is next, and it's where the magic happens. Vibrant visuals, enthralling videos, and engaging posts form the core of your strategy. Each piece of content must provide value, whether it's educational, inspiring, or entertaining. A mixture of formats will keep your audience intrigued and anticipating your next move.

But it's not just about what you post, it's also about when you post. Timing can dramatically affect the visibility and engagement of your content. Utilizing Facebook's insights to analyze when your audience is online can guide you to schedule posts for maximum impact.

Interactivity breeds loyalty. The more you engage with your audience—responding to comments, hosting live Q&A sessions, or running polls—the deeper the connection you forge. This engagement is the currency of the digital realm, and your return on investment can be substantial.

Let's not forget the aesthetic appeal of your page. A coherent visual theme can make your brand memorable. This could be through a consistent color scheme, a recurring graphic style, or the tone of your posts. A recognizable brand is a shareable brand, and shares translate into a broader audience.

Storytelling is also a powerful tool. Humans are innately drawn to stories, and Facebook provides the perfect platform for narrative content. Share your journey, the highs and lows, to create an emotional connection. Emotions drive shares, comments, and reactions, fueling the algorithms to favor your content.

Another pillar of a captivating Facebook presence is authenticity. In an online world filled with facades, be real. Authenticity forges a stronger, more genuine relationship with your audience, and people are more likely to invest in someone they trust.

Educate yourself on the latest trends and updates within Facebook. The platform is ever-changing, and staying ahead means you can capitalize on new features before they become oversaturated. Whether it's a new type of ad, a change in the algorithm, or a fresh content format, be an early adopter and ride the wave of innovation.

Facebook Groups are also an integral part of your empire-building. Groups foster community, allowing you to dive deeper into your niche and create a dedicated space for your followers to interact with each other. Leading a group also positions you as an authority in your space.

Don't underestimate the power of collaboration. Partner with other creators in your niche to cross-promote content. These partnerships can expose you to new audiences and also bring a fresh perspective to your existing followers.

Data should guide your decisions. Use analytics tools to monitor which types of content perform best. This isn't about chasing numbers but understanding what resonates with your audience so you can produce more of what they love.

Expand your presence beyond your page. Participate in relevant Facebook communities, comment on pages within your niche, and connect with your peers. Visibility outside your circle can attract new followers who stumble upon your insightful comments or shared wisdom.

Finally, infuse your personal brand into every facet of your Facebook presence. Your brand isn't just what you're selling or talking about—it's the sum of all interactions, visuals, and the tone you set. Embody your brand, and your Facebook empire will not just grow, but thrive.

Monetizing Your Facebook Audience

Having established an engaging Facebook presence, it's time to dive into the art of turning your audience into a reliable income source. This platform may seem casual and community-focused at first glance, but it's teeming with monetization prospects for those savvy enough to navigate its nuances. Whether you boast a sizeable followership eager to interact with your content or you're just starting to see engagement tick upward, there are strategies to cultivate that interest into steady earnings.

Note that the journey from a compelling Facebook presence to monetizing your audience isn't about instant gratification. It's an intricate dance of strategy, patience, and ingenuity. As you focus on harnessing the power of this platform, you'll discover that your efforts can lead to various streams of revenue.

Affiliate Marketing: If you've captivated your audience's trust, it's time to monetize that relationship. Affiliate marketing allows you to partner with businesses who will compensate you for promoting their products or services to your followers. Share personal anecdotes or creative content featuring those products, ensuring that each affiliate link serves as a seamless and sincere recommendation.

Exclusive Content and Subscriptions: With Facebook's subscription options, you can create an air of exclusivity while padding your purse. Entice fans with premium content they can't find anywhere else, and invite them to subscribe for a monthly fee. If you've been providing value consistently, your audience won't hesitate to get even more from you behind that velvet rope.

Facebook Ads: This is a powerful feature that can turbocharge your income. Strategically craft and place ads for your own offerings or external products that resonate with your followers. The key is to blend these promotions naturally within your normal content flow, making them helpful rather than obtrusive.

Product Sales: Use your page as a launchpad for your own products. Whether you're a wizard at creating digital guides or handcrafting artisanal goods, your Facebook audience is already primed for these offerings. Keep them engaged with sneak peeks, early bird offers, and behind-the-scenes looks at the creation process.

Sponsored Content: As your influence grows, brands may approach you to feature their products in your content. It's essential here to strike a balance between earning and authenticity. Choose sponsorships that align with your values and those of your community to both maintain trust and gain a reputation as a valued partner to brands.

Consider each of these avenues as weaving a rich tapestry of revenue—each thread complementing the other. Diversify your monetization methods to capitalize on the ebb and flow of online trends and consumer behavior. Investing in multiple streams of income will give you not only financial security but flexibility as well.

But remember, monetization is only part of the story. It needs to be approached with the same care and authenticity that helped you grow your following in the first place. Maintain the integrity of your content, be clear about sponsored posts, and never stop valuing the community you've built. This is how you turn a vibrant Facebook audience into a thriving, profitable empire.

From Likes to Loot: Strategies for Profit

Converting digital fans into a sustainable revenue stream may seem like alchemy, but with the right strategies, turning likes into loot is entirely possible. You're already building an engaged audience on Facebook; now it's time to leverage that loyalty and turn engagement into income. Every like, share, and comment can be a stepping stone towards a profitable business venture if you harness them effectively.

Firstly, let's talk direct sales. This immediate method involves selling products or services directly through your Facebook page. The platform's Shop feature allows users to browse and purchase without ever leaving Facebook, providing seamless transactions. But remember, high-quality visuals and compelling descriptions are crucial—use them as your virtual storefront display.

Next up is affiliate marketing. This entails promoting other brands' products and earning a commission on sales made through your unique referral link. Pin these links in your posts or include them in video descriptions. Strive for authenticity by recommending products you truly believe in—your audience's trust is your most valuable currency.

Can't get enough of advertising revenue? By joining the Facebook Audience Network, you can monetize your video content through ads. Make sure your videos are engaging and retain viewers, as this directly impacts your earnings. Optimize video content for the Facebook algorithm, keeping a close eye on watch times and engagement rates.

Let's remember the power of sponsorships. Companies are constantly seeking influencers with receptive audiences. Be proactive: put together a media kit that highlights your page's demographics and engagement rates. Show potential sponsors exactly why a partnership with you is an investment worth making. Remember, negotiation is key—don't sell yourself short.

Bringing in the power of crowdfunding, platforms like Patreon allow your most dedicated followers to support your creative endeavors for exclusive content or perks. Don't be afraid to be transparent about your goals and what the funding is for. Promote your membership platform regularly but tastefully across your social media outlets.

It's not all about posting, either. Hosting live events or webinars can be a lucrative venture. Use Facebook Live to engage with your audience in real-time and offer paid access to specialized content. This enriches your community relationship and creates a unique value proposition for your followers.

Perhaps digital products ignite your interest. Create and sell e-books, online courses, or downloadable guides. Once created, these assets require little upkeep but can generate income again and again. It's all about finding that sweet spot where your expertise meets your audience's needs.

While merchandise might seem old school, pairing physical products with your brand can be surprisingly profitable. Consider branded merchandise, whether it's apparel, mugs, or stickers, and utilize print-on-demand services to mitigate risk and inventory costs. Your brand loyalty can translate into a desire for tangible goods among your followers.

Not to ignore, paid subscriptions on Facebook can provide an additional income stream. Offer subscribers exclusive content or benefits. This constant revenue can stabilize your income, mitigating the unpredictable nature of advertising and affiliation earnings.

Don't overlook the importance of analytics. Monitor your progress, understand what works and what doesn't. Use insights to fine-tune your approach, track which types of monetization strategies resonate with your audience, and allocate your efforts accordingly. Being data-driven optimizes your revenue potential.

Additionally, collaboration amplifies profitability. Partner with fellow influencers or content creators to expand your reach. Joint ventures can lead to new audience members and fresh opportunities for monetization. Remember, there's strength in numbers.

But as you explore monetization, don't forget your community. Engage with your audience consistently. Ask for feedback, and let them feel part of the journey. Users who feel connected to your brand are far more likely to support your monetization endeavors.

Now, brace yourself for a bit of trial and error. Not every moneymaking strategy will yield immediate success, and that's okay. The digital landscape is ever-changing, and so should your methods. Be patient, stay innovative, and be willing to pivot when needed.

Finally, ensure you stay above board with advertising and sponsorship declarations—transparency is mandatory to maintain your reputation and abide by platform guidelines. Always keep abreast with the legalities of monetization to protect both yourself and your brand.

In wrapping up, transforming your Facebook presence into a profitable venture requires creativity, tenacity, and a strategic mindset. There's a wealth of potential at your fingertips, and with these strategies, you're well-equipped to tap into it. Forge ahead, the world of digital profit awaits. Acknowledge that with the right approach, you too can command the digital marketplace and claim your slice of the online prosperity.

Chapter 3:
Instagram Cash Flows: Capturing the Visual Market

Stepping into the Instagram arena is less like entering a boxing ring and more like joining a vibrant dance floor. This chapter is all focused on how you, with a keen eye for visuals and a strategic mind, can turn your Instagram account into a flourishing revenue stream. It's time to explore Instagram, an app with a billion-strong user base hungry for captivating content, and how you can carve out your slice of its vast economic pie.

Instagram's appeal lies in its simplicity and the potency of its visual storytelling. Every post you share is an opportunity to connect with an audience that's poised to engage, share, and respond — a goldmine for those looking to monetize their online presence. Yet, like any market worth its salt, capturing the visual market on Instagram requires finesse, intuition, and a solid game plan.

The Aesthetics of Income: Your Instagram Blueprint

First up, let's talk aesthetics. Instagram is the digital equivalent of window shopping; it's where your content needs to catch the eye, enchant the heart, and engage the mind, all in seconds. The quality of your visuals, coupled with the cohesiveness of your feed, are your first points of sale. Think of your Instagram feed as a gallery where every post contributes to a broader narrative about who you are and what value you bring to the table.

Once you understand the aesthetics, it's about leveraging Instagram's unique features — Stories, Reels, IGTV, and more — to build a dynamic presentation of your brand. Mastering each format's nuance isn't just a suggestion; it's necessary to captivate your audience in a variety of ways. This versatility shows sponsors you're capable of crafting compelling content that resonates with viewers, no matter the format.

Converting Followers Into Dollars

What's next after building an eye-catching feed? It's turning those avid scrollers into a source of income. Engagement is the currency of Instagram, and your ability to foster an active community can propel you from a simple user to a significant influencer. This paves the way for monetization techniques such as affiliate marketing, branded content, and even direct sales. Each interaction, each 'saved' post, each DM can signify a step toward financial success.

It's imperative that you understand the nuances of these strategies to utilize them to their full potential. Tagging products, creating shoppable posts, and leveraging analytics to understand your audience are all crucial steps. Cultivating relationships with your followers by consistently delivering value-laden content can elevate you from zero to hero in the Instagram income game.

Influencer Secrets: Partnerships and Sponsorships

Then we have the heavy-hitters: partnerships and sponsorships. Influencers reign supreme on Instagram, but what sets the successful ones apart is their knack for forging mutually beneficial relationships with brands. With every brand looking to tell a story, it's your job as an influencer to be the right storyteller for the right audience.

Navigating the world of partnerships requires a balance of assertiveness and authenticity. It's about pitching your unique voice and vision to brands that align with your values and following. The secret sauce? Understanding your worth and learning the art of negotiation. Armed with your engagement stats and a clear understanding of your impact, you'll be in a strong position to land deals that compliment your content and increase your cash flow.

As this chapter unfolds, we'll delve deeper into these facets of Instagram monetization, equipping you with actionable strategies and insights to turn your passion for visuals into a viable income. Keep your creative spark alight and your business mind sharp as we journey through the bustling bazaar that is Instagram. Your adventure in converting visual content into cash is just beginning, and the market awaits those ready to capture its attention.

The Aesthetics of Income: Your Instagram Blueprint

On the journey through the mosaic world of Instagram, aesthetics aren't just about beauty; they're the currency that can manifest into tangible income. This blueprint is your guide to transforming a visual platform into a profitable venture. Instagram remains a powerhouse in the universe of visual appeal, where each image or video can potentially seed a cash flow.

Firstly, recognize that your feed is your portfolio, your storefront, your brand. It's vital to curate your Instagram presence with intentionality, tuning into the visual desires of your target audience whilst remaining authentic to your personal brand. Every successful Instagram account is grounded in a strong, attractive aesthetic that captivates an audience and keeps them coming back for more.

Your blueprint begins with the cornerstone of any impactful Instagram account: consistency. Not just in posting schedule, but in the look and feel of your posts. Choose a color scheme or a set of filters that align with your brand's mood and stick to them. This visual cohesion will make your feed instantly recognizable to your followers, thereby strengthening your brand identity.

Next, consider the composition of your photos and videos. Are they structured in a way that leads your audience's eye through the story you're telling? Composition is key to making your content pop and stand out in a sea of endless scrolling. Use of space, symmetry, and framing all play a part in creating engaging content that pulls in viewers.

Content variety is also crucial to keeping your audience engaged while maintaining your aesthetic. Balance your feed with a mix of photos, carousel posts, videos, and Stories. Showcase your products or services, sure, but also give your followers a peek behind the curtain with behind-the-scenes content, user-generated features, and personal stories where appropriate.

Engagement on Instagram isn't just about visuals, though. Captions are your chance to infuse personality into your posts, to give context to your images, to engage directly with your audience. They should be as carefully crafted as your images, honed to spark conversation, share insights, or provide value. Craft your captions to speak to your ideal customer, and don't forget to include a call-to-action where relevant.

Hashtags are often an untapped treasure trove when it comes to reaching new audiences on Instagram. While aesthetics draw people in, the right hashtags make sure they find you in the first place. Curate your hashtags to speak to your niche market and check the performance of different hashtags to adjust your strategy accordingly.

Storytelling through Instagram can't be overstated in its importance. Each post should contribute to a broader narrative, one that aligns with your brand's values and mission. Followers should be able to sense your passion for whatever your brand represents, whether that's the latest fashion trends, innovative tech gadgets, or awe-inspiring travel locations.

Your blueprint also includes mastering the art of Instagram Stories and Highlights. These features offer a dynamic way to present content that might not fit into your feed's aesthetic. Use Stories to post real-time updates, host Q&As, or share spontaneous moments, using Highlights to create a permanent home for this content on your profile.

Leveraging Instagram's various shopping features can turn your aesthetics into a direct shopping experience. If you're selling a product, tag it in your posts and stories to provide an easy path for impulse buys. This seamless integration between showcasing your product and making a sale is crucial in converting followers into customers.

In the realm of Instagram, analytics should become your best friend. Regularly review your insights to understand what type of content resonates most with your audience. Which posts garner the most engagement? What time does your audience interact with your content the most? Use this data to refine your strategy and maximize your income potential.

Collaborations and partnerships, meanwhile, can enhance your aesthetic and expand your reach. A smart collaboration with another Instagrammer or brand can expose your profile to new potential followers and customers. Ensure that any collaboration fits within the aesthetic of your brand and brings value to your audience.

Don't underestimate the value of quality when it comes to the visuals you post. Investing in a good camera or editing software can make a remarkable difference in the quality of your content, setting you apart from competitors. Remember, in the age of high resolutions and crystal-clear displays, the standard for quality content is constantly rising. Be ready to meet it.

Finally, don't forget that your journey on Instagram is one of constant learning and adaptation. The platform evolves, trends come and go, and what works today may not work tomorrow. Stay agile, keep learning, and never be afraid to pivot your strategy. By marrying your unique aesthetic to a strategic approach, you can tap into Instagram's vast potential for generating income.

Embrace the philosophy that each square on your Instagram grid represents an opportunity to connect, to inspire, and to monetize. Your success will be a reflection of your commitment to understanding what visuals resonate in the current market and how to link those to the value you offer. With the right aesthetic, your Instagram blueprint is not just a map, but a compelling visual story that leads to financial reward.

Converting Followers Into Dollars

Having amassed a loyal following on Instagram, it's now time to transform this digital goldmine into a lucrative stream of income. After all, a follower count is much more than a vanity metric; it's a bustling marketplace, teeming with untapped financial potential that is ripe for the harvesting.

But how does one translate a number into currency? It's about creating and delivering value that resonates with your audience so deeply that they are willing to open their wallets for it. It's not just about pushing products or counting on sponsored posts, it's about strategic engagement and crafting an irresistible offer that your followers simply can't overlook.

Understand Your Audience

First, get to know your audience like the back of your hand. What links them together? What do they seek in the content they consume? This understanding is the cornerstone of a conversion-ready Instagram presence. Tailor your content to match what makes your followers tick, and they'll feel more connected to your brand – and more inclined to support it financially.

Provide Genuine Value

It's crucial that you start by providing genuine value. Before you ask for anything, ensure you've given plenty – whether it's entertainment, information, or inspiration. This balance creates a rapport and sets the stage for financial transactions that feel more like mutual exchanges rather than a hard sell.

Engage With Purpose

Next, engage with purpose. Active, meaningful engagement builds trust and rapport. When followers comment, make them feel heard. When they share or save your posts, acknowledge their support. This sense of community not only fosters loyalty but primes your audience for future offers and promotions.

Monetize With Integrity

To convert followers into dollars, striking the right chord with monetization is essential. Affiliate marketing, sponsored content, and selling your own products or services are all proven methods. Choose those that align with your brand and audience tastes. When done with integrity and transparency, monetization builds your brand equity rather than undercutting it.

Exclusive Offers

Create exclusive offers that make your followers feel special — limited-time discounts, early access to products, or members-only content. An offer they can't find anywhere else is incredibly compelling, spurring followers to take action.

Diversify Your Revenue Streams

Diversify your revenue streams to ensure stability in your financial influx. Relying on a single source is a gamble. Instead, mix direct sales, sponsored content, and other channels to build a resilient revenue model that withstands the ebb and flow of platform trends and policy changes.

Track and Adapt

Lastly, measure your success and adapt as necessary. Track which types of content drive the most conversions and refine your strategy to capitalize on what works. Stay aware of changing trends and be nimble enough to pivot your approach when necessary to keep the cash flowing.

Remember, the secret sauce in converting followers into dollars is a blend of authenticity, strategy, and hard work. Your Instagram platform is more than just a collection of images; it's a curated experience that, when leveraged with savvy and heart, can yield handsome financial rewards.

Influencer Secrets: Partnerships and Sponsorships

As an influencer, discovering the power of partnerships and sponsorships might just be the most pivotal moment in your journey to monetizing your online presence. It's here, in the art of collaboration, that the potential for real, substantial income resides. Navigating this arena requires both savvy negotiation skills and an understanding of your own worth. But let's break it down into actionable steps, insights, and strategies.

You've laid a strong foundation through your content, and you've cultivated an engaged audience on platforms like Instagram; now it's time to channel this into lucrative partnerships with brands. Begin with pinpointing companies aligned with your values and aesthetic. A seamless fit ensures authenticity—a crucial component your followers can sense.

Your pitch to potential sponsors should tell a compelling story—why you and why your audience? Here's where you leverage your uniqueness. Highlight demographics, engagement rates, and any success stories of past collaborations. Quantifying your influence makes you impossible to ignore.

Once you've caught the eye of a brand, it's crucial to negotiate terms that respect your influence. Don't sell yourself short. Recognize that your voice has power, and your platform provides a valuable service. Your rate should reflect the quality and reach of your work.

Transparency with your audience is key when introducing sponsored content. Followers prize honesty, and forthright disclosure of partnerships not only fulfills legal obligations but cultivates trust. And in the digital realm, trust translates into sustained engagement and growth.

An influencer's toolkit must include media kits and rate cards—essentials for communicating your value proposition. They should be polished, professional, and up-to-date, exemplifying your brand and what you stand for. This material is often your first impression; make it count.

Long-term partnerships can be more beneficial than one-off deals. They provide stability and the opportunity for creative growth. Aim for these by proving ROI from past initiatives. Brands are more likely to invest over time if you've delivered results and demonstrated commitment.

Yet, it's not just about large brands. Micro-influencers often thrive by tapping into local or niche markets, forming partnerships with small businesses that resonate with their community. The key is relevance and resonance with your audience. Deliver that, and you create value for everyone involved.

Don't underestimate the power of collaboration with other influencers. Joint campaigns can double the exposure and breathe new life into your content. More importantly, they can introduce you to new segments of an audience primed for what you have to offer.

Sponsorship contracts can be dense and complex. Always scrutinize the fine print before signing. If in doubt, seek professional advice. Your content—and control over it—along with payment terms and deliverables should be crystal clear to avoid future misunderstandings.

In an age where influence is currency, diversification is key. Don't put all your eggs in one basket. Leverage your influence through multiple partnerships. This not just minimizes risks but also broadens your earning potential across various industries and audiences.

Measure, evaluate, and iterate. The effectiveness of sponsored posts should be gauged meticulously through engagement metrics and conversion rates. This information isn't just crucial for your own strategic adjustments—it's concrete proof of your value to current and future partners.

Beyond direct sponsorships, affiliate programs can supplement influencer income smartly. By earning commissions on product sales through your unique codes or links, you blend organic content with subtle promotion—a win-win for you and the brand.

Innovation in partnership approaches sets influencers apart. Virtual events, giveaways, and personalized promotions capture attention and drive engagement. Be the catalyst that sparks interaction between brands and your audience, and watch partnerships flourish.

Ultimately, the influencer life is not just about taking snapshots and posting updates. It's about crafting a sustainable business model.

Partnerships and sponsorships can provide the financial backbone for this model, but it's your drive, creativity, and strategic thinking that will make it thrive. So don't just aim to influence—aspire to innovate and lead in the ever-evolving world of social media.

Chapter 4:
Mastering Threads: The Untapped Goldmine

In the vast landscape of social media platforms, there's a potent resource often overlooked by those seeking online income: Threads. This interactive tool resides within the borders of your favorite social platforms, weaving a fabric that can hold the golden keys to unlocking new revenue streams. Let's delve into why Threads are more than just digital conversations—they're a treasure trove waiting for the savvy user to mine.

The art of mastering Threads lies in leveraging them beyond their basic function of communication. A well-utilized Thread can boost your visibility, establish your expertise, and create a dedicated community around your brand. But how can you turn these strings of messages into gold?

Understanding Threads and Its Earning Potential

At first glance, Threads may seem like just another way to respond to comments or inquiries. However, by actively engaging in these micro-dialogues, you're building a rapport with your audience. People feel heard and valued when you interact with them directly. This connection fosters trust, and trust is a currency in the online world that can be transformed into income. Picture this: each response is a potential seed that, with care and attention, can grow into a customer, client, or business opportunity.

Navigating the Do's and Don'ts of Threads Engagement

To tap into the power of Threads, it's important to understand the do's and don'ts. Do be authentic and relatable; your replies should feel as though they're coming from a friend. This means using a natural tone, avoiding overly salesy language, and showing that you genuinely care about the conversation.

Don't fall into the trap of scattering generic replies. Each interaction within a Thread should be unique, reflecting that you've considered the individual's comment or question. Keep in mind that quality trumps quantity—you're crafting a narrative that people want to follow, not merely padding your reply count.

Whether you're unraveling the complexities of a subject within a Thread, solving a problem, or adding thoughtful insights, each contribution solidifies your standing as a thought leader. And as this influence grows, so does your capacity to monetize your expertise.

Imagine transforming a discussion on the latest tech gadget into a series of affiliate sales, or turning a debate on the best yoga practices into a full-fledged online course, with Threads serving as both the classroom and the marketing platform. The path from conversations to cash is paved with the gold of your knowledge and the strength of your relationships.

In this chapter, you've begun to uncover just why Threads are such an untapped goldmine. They are more than tools for engagement; they're the connective tissue between you and your next successful venture. By mastering Threads, you harness the capability to enrich not only your audience's experience but also your own financial well-being.

Remember, while Threads may appear to be a normal feature of social media life, for the discerning entrepreneur, they are vibrant ecosystems, brimming with opportunities. Navigate them with intention, participate with passion, and watch as the threads you weave turn to gold.

Understanding Threads and Its Earning Potential

In the ever-expanding universe of social media, the savvy explorer is constantly on the lookout for new territories to conquer. Amongst these, a new horizon is emerging, rich with potential yet largely untapped: the world of "Threads." But what exactly is meant by "Threads," and how can their leverage translate into tangible earnings for you? Let's unravel this mystery together.

Firstly, let's clarify our terminology. Threads, in the context of social media, refer to a series of connected posts on platforms such as Twitter, Reddit, or even in the comments section of Instagram and Facebook. They string together narratives, discussions, and content in a way that hooks readers and encourages engagement. This connectivity not only sustains interest but also builds community—a foundational currency in the digital realm.

Understanding the earning potential of Threads begins with recognizing their power to amplify your reach. Each contribution to a thread can draw in new eyes, affixed to the unfolding story or discussion. This is where the potential lies: the more engagement your threads generate, the more attractive you become to brands and businesses looking for influential personalities to promote their products.

Sourcing income from threads isn't a casual stroll in the park; it demands strategy. The magic brew for profitability lies within the potion of high-quality content, consistent engagement, and shrewd networking. By positioning yourself as a provider of valuable insights or entertainment, you can start building a following that looks forward to each installment of your threaded content.

An advantage threads hold over standalone posts is their inherent nature of continued storytelling. They compel audience return, fostering a sense of anticipation. This regularity and predictability can be monetized through several avenues, including affiliate marketing, sponsored content, and direct promotions—all of which revolve around weaving the thread of your narrative with subtle calls to action.

A prime example of thread monetization is leveraging affiliate marketing within your narratives. By embedding affiliate links within your threads, you encourage followers to make purchases or sign up for services, for which you receive a commission. The continuity and context provided by threads enhance the likelihood of these links being clicked, as opposed to random promotion.

Sponsorships, too, are a gold mine for thread maestros. Brands value the intimate and authentic nature of a well-crafted thread. By sharing stories or discussions that naturally incorporate a sponsor's product, you're not just advertising—you're integrating, which translates to value for both your audience and the sponsor.

Beyond just promoting products, your sought-after thread presence can lead you to paid partnerships with brands. Imagine crafting a thread that aligns so seamlessly with a brand's identity that they pay you not only for product placement but also for your skill in engaging the audience and maintaining loyalty.

Networking also plays a pivotal role in cultivating your threads' earning potential. Each interaction is a bridge to new opportunities, from collaborations with fellow content creators to invitations to exclusive events—which, in turn, can facilitate even deeper brand relationships and partnerships.

Consider too the sale of your own products or content. A compelling thread can be the ideal runway for launching your offerings. Here, the trust you've built with your narrative skills becomes the perfect setting to present your merchandise, courses, or premium content to a keen and receptive audience.

The beauty of threads is that their efficacy is not contingent on having a massive following. Engagement is the key metric here, and a small but active community can sometimes outperform larger, more passive ones. This makes threads an especially lucrative tool for those just stepping into the social media game.

Remember, the power of threads lies in the human connection they foster. They allow for a deeper dive into topics, prompting discussion and consideration. This emotional investment translates into a powerful marketing tool that can sway opinions and open wallets.

To tap into the earning potential of threads, it's crucial to refine your storytelling abilities and understand the nuances of each social media platform. Threads work differently on Twitter, where brevity reigns supreme, compared to Instagram, where visuals take the lead. Tailoring your approach to each platform's unique language is part of mastering this craft.

Lastly, there's longevity to consider. Well-constructed threads can continue to generate income long after their creation. Due to their engaging nature, they can keep resurfacing, sometimes going viral, long after you've woven their tale. This evergreen potential creates a compounding effect, contributing to a sustainable income stream over time.

In the chapters that follow, we'll guide you into the heart of these strategies, exploring the do's and don'ts of thread engagement and tapping into their full potential. Mastering threads could very well be the catalyst in transforming your social media presence from a pastime into a profitable venture. As you delve into the craft, remember that every word you thread can be a step closer to wealth in this digital goldmine.

Navigating the Do's and Don'ts of Threads Engagement

As we peered into the enticing world of Threads and its earning potential in the previous chapter, we've now arrived at a vital junction: understanding the delicate art of Threads engagement. It's a brilliant canvas where each stroke contributes to your masterpiece of online success. Let's navigate these waters with a savvy mind, ensuring each move we make solidifies our journey to financial freedom.

Engagement on Threads, whether it's Facebook, Instagram, or specialized platforms, demands a nuanced approach. It's not merely posting content; it's about fostering a community that actively participates in the dialogue you initiate. The key is balance. Too little interaction, and your thread remains unnoticed; too much, and you risk turning your audience away.

Starting with the do's, remember that authenticity rules. As you weave stories and share content, always imbue it with a genuine touch of your personality. People aren't just buying into a product or service; they're investing in you. Let your unique light shine through your Threads to establish a connection that transcends transactions.

Furthermore, be prompt and present in your interactions. Timely responses to comments or inquiries don't just boost engagement metrics; they portray a portrait of dedication and attentiveness. This is the digital equivalent of a warm handshake or a reassuring smile – it builds a rapport that can convert followers into loyal customers.

Another critical do is consistency. This doesn't mean bombarding your audience with content, but rather establishing a rhythm that they can anticipate and look forward to. Like the ebb and flow of the ocean, your consistent presence should be comforting, not overwhelming.

Now, moving to the don'ts, steer clear of inflammatory or divisive content. Threads should be a place where positive exchange thrives. While controversy can sometimes spark engagement, it's often detrimental in the long term. Keep your eyes on the prize – a cohesive community that supports your financial aspirations, not a battleground of ideologies.

Resist using engagement baiting tactics that beg for likes, shares, or follows. This can be seen as disingenuous and often backfires by alienating your audience. Instead, foster a natural inclination for your followers to engage by creating irresistible content.

Where possible, don't just talk at your community; talk with them. Engagement is a two-way street. Ask questions, solicit opinions, and invite your audience into your creative process. By doing so, you're not just building a fanbase; you're nurturing a fellowship of participants in your success story.

Regarding content, avoid recycling the same themes repetitively. Innovation is your ally in the Threads universe. Keep your content fresh and exciting, stoking the fires of curiosity amongst your viewers. Remember, predictability is the antithesis of fascination.

Be wary of overselling. While monetization is your goal, your audience should never feel like just a means to an end. Instead, let your products or services seamlessly integrate into the value you're consistently providing. It's about creating an environment where sales are the natural next step for your engaged community.

Lastly, never neglect the power of analytics. Engagement isn't just a feeling; it's measurable. Failure to monitor and adapt to the insights provided by analytical tools is like sailing without a compass. The numbers tell a story of what resonates and what falls flat. Heed their narrative to adjust your strategies accordingly.

In a realm where the competition is but a click away, standing out takes an artful blend of tactics and authenticity. Through understanding the do's and don'ts of Threads engagement, you're not just shooting arrows in the dark; you're an astute archer hitting mark after mark.

Whether a seasoned navigator or a newcomer charting the digital waters, the principles of engagement remain constant. Blend your content with sincerity, maintain a respectful and interactive community, and keep a meticulous eye on the pulse of your audience's reactions.

As you continue to dabble in the rich prospects of social media, let the wisdom of strategic Threads engagement guide you. It's not just about riding the waves; it's about being the wave that others are drawn to. Remember, at the heart of every successful online endeavor, is an engaged and thriving community, intricately woven by the deft hands of an attentive creator.

So, harness the power of engagement, and watch as your Threads transform into the golden strands of your online income tapestry. It's here, within this labyrinth of connections and interactions, that the untapped goldmine of social media truly reveals itself.

Chapter 5:
The TikTok Takeover: Short Videos, Big Bucks

In the whirlwind world of social media, a new giant has emerged, commanding global attention with its short yet captivating video content. TikTok's meteoric rise to stardom has opened up unprecedented opportunities for savvy individuals to tap into a goldmine of online earnings. This chapter unravels the secrets to not just riding the TikTok wave, but mastering it to garner fame and fortune from the comfort of your screen.

TikTok Basics for Viral Success

Understanding the core mechanisms of TikTok is essential for anyone trying to harness its income-generating power. You've got to know the ins and outs, from creating an engaging profile to deciphering the trends that could take your content viral. Getting a grip on basics such as seamless editing, eye-catching visuals, and strategic content timing can set the stage for your TikTok triumph.

Imagine yourself as a maestro, and your TikTok account is the orchestra. Every element must be in tune with the platform's dynamic rhythm. You can capitalize on your creativity, crafting short, impactful videos that resonate with millions, all while optimizing your content to meet the fickle favors of the TikTok algorithm.

Monetizing Trends: Beyond Dancing Clips

Now, you might think TikTok is all about dance challenges, lip-syncing, and comedic skits. However, it's only the surface. Beyond the entertainment lies a fertile landscape for monetization. Are you an expert at DIY crafts? Can you offer quick fitness tips or have a knack for simplifying complex concepts? There's a place for your skill set in TikTok's diverse ecosystem. By identifying and tailoring your content to your niche, you can attract a dedicated audience that is not just engaged but also willing to open their wallets.

With the right approach, you can transform your TikTok presence into a lucrative income source. Brand partnerships, live stream gifts, merchandise promotions, and even TikTok's own Creator Fund ensure that content creators are remunerated for their viral sensations.

The Algorithm Advantage: Timing and Hashtags

Cracking the code of TikTok's algorithm is like finding the secret sauce to online virality. This platform rewards those who understand the intricate dance of timing, trends, and hashtags. By aligning your content's release with peak user activity times and hitching your posts to the day's trending hashtags, you're much more likely to see your views—and your potential earnings—skyrocket.

Elevate your TikTok game by utilizing analytics to your advantage, iterating on success patterns in your content, and staying ahead of the curve when it comes to platform updates and feature releases. Mastery of these elements is not just recommended; it's a must for anyone serious about making significant income on this rapidly evolving platform.

The stage is set, the audience awaits, and the potential for profit is just a viral hit away. With TikTok's highly engaged community, the impact of your creative endeavors is limited only by your imagination and willingness to learn the ropes. Forge your path in the TikTok domain, where short videos can indeed lead to big bucks.

TikTok Basics for Viral Success

In the dynamic digital era of 'scroll and like', TikTok has emerged as a front-runner, setting the pace for short-form video content that hooks viewers in merely seconds. If you're looking to ride the TikTok wave straight to the bank, understanding the platform's nuts and bolts is crucial. We're diving into the essentials for viral magic on TikTok, and how you can transform that magic into monetary success.

Firstly, let's talk about the heartbeat of TikTok - its algorithm. It's a blend of recency, user interaction, video information, and device/account settings. To make it work for you, crafting content that resonates with your intended audience is vital. But where do you start? It begins with trend-spotting. Being on the pulse of what's hot can give your content a fighting chance to be seen by the masses.

Virality on TikTok often hinges on relatability and replication. Challenges, dance routines, and catchy soundbites are content gold. Position yourself as a trendsetter or be an early adopter of emerging trends to maximize exposure. A knack for trendspotting can elevate your content from being seen by a few to being replicated by thousands. Remember, timing is everything - capitalize on trends at their inception.

Creating content isn't just about following trends. It's also about innovation. Put your own twist on what's going around. Authenticity is engaging, and it's the original takes on a popular trend that often rise to the top. Encourage interaction by making your content something viewers can participate in or respond to - engagement is currency in the TikTok economy.

Now, let's talk aesthetics. Your videos should pop. Use TikTok's myriad of filters, effects, and editing tools to craft a visual feast. Sharp visuals coupled with high-quality audio are more likely to keep a viewer gripped long enough for the TikTok algorithm to take notice. Remember, your first few seconds are critical - make them count!

Audio on TikTok isn't just background noise; it's a cornerstone of the platform. Utilizing trending sounds can boost your content's discoverability. Pair captivating visuals with the perfect sound, and you've got a recipe for content that sticks. Pay attention to the 'For You' page to identify what audio tracks are currently under the spotlight.

Hashtags are the signposts that guide users to your content. Using a combination of broad and niche hashtags can improve your chances of appearing on desired 'For You' pages. But refrain from cluttering with irrelevant tags - TikTok's smarter than that and may penalize you for it.

Engagement doesn't end with your content's final frame. Interact with your followers through comments, duets, and stitches. The more you engage, the more you encourage your viewers to keep the conversation going. It's a two-way street - show your audience that you value their time and attention.

Consistency is your friend on TikTok. Establishing a posting schedule not only keeps you disciplined but also builds anticipation within your audience. However, don't sacrifice quality for quantity. While more content increases visibility, subpar videos may damage your reputation over time.

User behavior analytics can become your best strategy tool. TikTok provides a wealth of data – use it. Look at who's watching and engaging with your videos. Tailor your content to your audience's preferences by analyzing what's working and what's not. It's like a continuous feedback loop that refines your content strategy with precision.

Collaborations can catapult your reach far beyond your current audience. Teaming up with other creators, especially those in a similar niche, introduces you to new audiences that might stay for your content. Partnerships are mutually beneficial - they share your genius with their followers, and you return the favor.

Believe in the content you create or no one else will. Your passion needs to bleed through your videos. Audiences can sense inauthenticity, and nothing turns a viewer off faster than a creator who doesn't resonate with their own message. Authenticity breeds loyalty, and a loyal audience is the bedrock of any successful TikTok channel.

Remember, while viral videos are great for short-term spikes in viewership, your goal is to convert those viewers into long-term followers. Offer value, whether it's through entertainment, information, or a captivating narrative. When followers see the value you add to their TikTok experience, they'll stick around – and it's those long-term followers who'll contribute to your financial success on the platform.

Last but not least, don't put all your eggs in one content basket. Experiment with different video formats and styles. You never know which one might resonate with an untapped audience segment. TikTok is all about creativity, so let yours shine across various content types to see which yields the best engagement and growth.

Reaching TikTok success is a blend of strategic planning, content innovation, and authentic engagement. By mastering the platform's basics and applying them with a unique flair, you can set yourself on a pathway not just to viral fame but also to substantial financial gain. Harness the power of TikTok, and you might just find yourself at the helm of an incredibly lucrative venture, all from the palm of your hand.

Monetizing Trends: Beyond Dancing Clips

So you've seen the catchy rhythms and grooves leading to online stardom, but let's push past the surface and dive deeper into the plethora of opportunities that TikTok offers for monetization. Indeed, while dance challenges are a staple of the platform, they barely scratch the surface of its potential to craft lucrative content. Consider this: Every niche, no matter how narrow, has an audience on TikTok waiting to engage with content that strikes a chord.

Moving beyond dancing clips means tapping into unique trends and creating content that not only entertains but also educates, inspires, or solves a problem for your viewers. Think of DIY tutorials, life hacks, personal finance tips, or even language learning bites. Each of these content types gives you a chance to deliver value in a way that captures attention and can seamlessly integrate with brands and affiliate marketing opportunities.

Remember, TikTok's algorithm favors content that generates strong engagement, so pinpointing what resonates with your audience can transform your feed into a magnet for potential partnerships. Savvy creators are leveraging their expertise, whether it's in fashion, tech, cooking, or fitness, and attracting sponsors who crave the spotlight that a thriving TikTok presence can provide.

For instance, if you're into tech, consider doing flash reviews of the latest gadgets or quick how-to guides for common software troubles. These pieces of content are not only helpful but have the potential to be shared widely, tapping into TikTok's viral nature. And with such content, you can attract tech brands looking for authentic advocates of their products.

Furthermore, don't underestimate the power of storytelling. Emotional and relatable stories can have a massive impact, leading to a loyal following that's more likely to support crowdfunded projects or buy merchandise. And if you align with a trending social cause, the potential for content to resonate and spread is enormous, opening doors to collaborations with non-profits and socially-conscious brands.

And let's not forget educational content - it's a gold mine on TikTok. Quick, digestible tips related to science, history, or even math can catch on like wildfire if presented in an engaging manner. Educators and experts can monetize by offering in-depth learning through external platforms or resources while using TikTok clips as their primary vehicle for outreach and connection.

Ultimately, the key is to think creatively about the type of content that aligns with your interests and expertise, while also considering the trends that TikTok audiences gravitate toward. When these elements align, you're not just participating in trends, you're setting them - creating a unique space for yourself that's ripe for monetization.

The Algorithm Advantage: Timing and Hashtags

Unlocking the potential of TikTok's algorithm is like cracking the code to a safe filled with endless opportunities. When utilized correctly, the timing of your posts and the strategic use of hashtags can catapult your content to viral status and pave the way for substantial online earnings.

Understanding TikTok's algorithm is key to success on the platform. It's designed to showcase content that it believes users will find engaging. This means that the timing of your posts can significantly influence how much exposure your content receives. Uploading videos when your audience is most active increases the likelihood of higher engagement, which, in turn, can result in the TikTok algorithm favoring your content.

Research shows that there are peak times during the day when users are more likely to be scrolling through TikTok. By studying analytics and observing global trends, you can pinpoint these golden hours. Generally, early mornings, lunchtime hours, and evenings are prime times for posting, but it's essential to test and adapt to your specific audience's habits.

Equally important to timing is the savvy use of hashtags. Hashtags are the compasses that guide users to your content amidst a sea of endless videos. They function as the connectors between your content and your intended audience. Using trending and relevant hashtags can amplify your reach by making your videos more discoverable.

Blend popular hashtags with more niche ones to cast a wide yet targeted net. This mix helps you to achieve visibility while also reaching audiences that are specifically interested in the content you're offering. Don't forget to monitor what's trending on TikTok's Discover page. Jumping on these trends early can give your content a significant boost.

Creating a unique hashtag for your brand or campaign can bolster your marketing efforts. When followers use your hashtag, it creates a ripple effect, multiplying your content's reach beyond your own followers. It lays the groundwork for a community or movement that your content is at the center of.

Avoid the temptation to flood your posts with an excessive number of hashtags. TikTok's algorithm could perceive this as spammy behavior. Instead, keep it focused and relevant. Typically, between three to five carefully chosen hashtags will suffice.

Engage with trends, but do so with a creative twist. The algorithm favors uniqueness, so while you may use trending hashtags, give the trend your spin. This not only keeps your content fresh but also showcases your creativity to the TikTok community, further boosting engagement.

Besides using hashtags, leveraging the algorithm involves interacting with other TikTok users. Commenting on videos, responding to comments on your own content, and participating in challenges and duets show the algorithm that you are an active member of the community. This interaction can lead to increased visibility of your posts.

Remember, hashtags and timing are not static strategies. TikTok's platform is dynamic, and trends can rise and fall within hours. Staying informed and adapting to changes ensures that your strategy remains effective. Continually analyze your performance, and don't be afraid to tweak your approach.

Now, imagine the feeling of seeing your content snowball into a viral sensation, all because you played your cards right with timing and hashtags. The algorithm can be your best ally in your journey to making money online through TikTok. But it demands a careful balance of strategic planning, attentiveness to trends, and adaptability.

For instance, you might notice that posts tagged with a certain hashtag perform better on weekdays. Use this insight to inform your posting schedule, ensuring your content aligns with peak engagement times for that specific conversation or interest.

Hashtags and timing are just part of the equation. Remember to also provide value in every piece of content you create. The TikTok community gravitates towards authenticity, entertainment, and usefulness. When you pair valuable content with strategic hashtag and timing choices, you'll find yourself on the fast track to building a profitable online presence.

Patience and persistence are your virtues here. Not every video will be a hit, and that's okay. With each upload, you're learning and evolving your strategy. The algorithm is like a river, ever-changing, and your job is to navigate its currents. Stay the course, and soon enough, you'll find the winning combination that sends your content and earnings flowing.

Go ahead, harness the algorithm advantage with intelligence and foresight. As you synchronize your timing and craft your hashtags with intention, you're setting the stage for your most lucrative clicks, views, and ultimately, profit. The virtual stage of TikTok awaits, and it's your time to shine.

Chapter 6:
Going Viral: Your Blueprint for Social Media Fame

You've been discovering the landscapes of social media, learning its wealth-generating terrain, from the kingdom of Facebook to the visual realms of Instagram, threading through Threads, and gyrating to the zeitgeist of TikTok. It's now time to bring this adventure to a peak. Yes, we're talking about the coveted viral sensation that can escalate you to social media fame and fortune.

The Virality Factor: What Makes Content Spread

Imagine creating content that ripples across the social media ocean, catching wave after wave of shares, likes, and comments. That's the dream, and here's your map: Virality isn't a fluke; it's a concoction of relatability, emotion, and a sprinkle of good timing. A dash of humor, a riveting story, or inspiration can be your ticket in. But remember, it's all about striking a chord with your audience, giving them not just something to engage with, but something to rally behind.

Understanding your audience is essential. You've got to know what makes them tick, what they adore, and what content they can't help but spread like wildfire. Research topics that resonate, trends that tantalize, and narratives that nudge people to hit that share button. Let your creativity flow, align it with your users' heartbeat, and you're on the right path to virality.

Leveraging Viral Content for Maximum Earnings

Now that you've got the secret sauce to virality, let's turn those views into value, that stardom into a steady income. When your content breaks the internet's sound barrier, advertisers and brands take notice. That's your cue to negotiate sponsorships, mature your merchandise line, or enhance your affiliate marketing game. Every view can turn into a cent, every share into a sale.

Think of viral content as a spotlight, illuminating your brand, your message, and your offerings. It's the perfect stage to highlight your products, showcase your services, or direct traffic to monetized platforms. But act swiftly; the viral window can be brief. Make sure you have your monetization mechanisms in place to capitalize on the surge before it ebbs away.

Remember, virality isn't just a quick hit of fame; it's an opportunity to establish credibility, grow a devoted following, and lay the foundation for long-term success. As you ferment excitement with each viral hit, stay true to your brand, and your audience will stick with you, from viral to vital.

In essence, your content doesn't have to just go viral; it should carry your signature, a part of you that resonates and reacts with the social media ecosystem to yield a bounty of engagements and earnings. With vigilance, versatility, and a touch of viral wizardry, the blueprint to social media fame is right here in your hands.

The Virality Factor: What Makes Content Spread

Understanding the virality factor is crucial in your quest for social media fame, and grasping this can make the difference between obscurity and stardom. Let's delve into the elements that can propel your content into the viral stratosphere. One major factor is the relatability of your content. When people see themselves in your content or it strikes a familiar chord, they are far more likely to share it with their friends and followers.

Emotion also drives shareability, so creating content that evokes strong reactions, whether it's joy, surprise, or even sadness, is powerful. However, be sure to lean towards positive emotions, as these are more likely to encourage sharing and engagement. The positivity of your content can become a beacon that draws in viewers from all corners of the internet.

Another key component is the element of surprise. If your content is unexpected or provides a twist, viewers are enticed to share the surprise with others. Who doesn't love being the first to show friends something astonishing or hilarious? This factor can turn a simple piece of content into a shared experience that ripples through the social media ecosystem. Keep them guessing, and they'll reward you with their shares.

While these emotional and psychological triggers are potent, we can't ignore the practical side of viral content: simplicity and shareability. Your content needs to be easy to consume and even easier to share. Complex messages or convoluted sharing processes will only hinder your spread potential, so ensure your call-to-action is as simple as 'click share.'

Timing also plays a pivotal role in content virality. Capitalize on current events, trends, or memes to position your content within the larger social conversation. By tapping into the zeitgeist, you ensure your content rides the wave of relevance and garners more attention than it might otherwise receive.

Let's not forget the power of a good story. Humans are hardwired to love narratives. Craft content that tells a compelling story, and you're likely to see your view counts soar as people are drawn into the narrative and eager to share it with others.

Networking with influencers or other content creators can amplify your viral potential exponentially. Collaborations or simply getting a shoutout from a well-established social media personality can skyrocket your content's exposure. Foster relationships within the influencer community, as these can be your gateways to a wider audience.

Utility cannot be overlooked either. If your content is useful, such as a life hack or an educational piece, it provides immediate value to the viewer, which can be a significant motivator for sharing. People love to be the bearers of useful information, so give them something worthwhile to pass along.

Exclusivity can also add to your content's virality. If you can offer content that can't be found anywhere else, or provide early access to information or products, viewers will share simply to be part of the exclusive group that 'knows.' By crafting unique content, you're not just creating; you're giving your audience a VIP pass.

Interactive and participatory content invites your audience to be a part of the creation itself. This can range from challenges, contests, or calls for user-generated content. When your followers become creators, they're more invested in the content and more likely to spread the word.

Aesthetics also have their say in the viral game. Your content needs to look good. Invest time into making your visuals appealing, as eye-catching images or slick videos are more likely to be shared. In a sea of content, those that stand out visually are the ones that rise to the top.

Of course, none of this matters if you don't understand the platform you're using. Each social media site has its own culture and algorithm. Tailor your content to fit within these parameters, and don't be afraid to experiment to see what works best. The right piece of content on the right platform at the right time can be a recipe for virality.

The element of interactivity should not be overlooked. Engaging with your audience through comments, live streams, or direct messages not only builds a community around your content but also encourages viewers to become advocates for your brand, magnifying your reach.

The virality factor isn't a one-size-fits-all formula, but rather a blend of art and science. It's about crafting content that resonates, engages, and inspires your audience to act. As you continue to refine your approach, stay adaptable and observe what's working. Learn from each post, and apply those lessons to your next piece of content.

Remember, at the heart of virality is the understanding that we are all seeking connection. Create content that bridges gaps, brings smiles, or enlightens, and you tap into the fundamental human desire to share experiences with others. As you set forth on your viral journey, keep the human element at the center of your content—it's the true essence of the virality factor.

Leveraging Viral Content for Maximum Earnings

In the exhilarating world of social media, going viral is the modern-day gold rush. It's a phenomenon that can catapult you from obscurity to fame—giving you substantial earning potential overnight. But what happens after your content hits the high marks of shares and likes? It's pivotal to know the next steps to ensure that your viral moment turns into a lasting income. In the competitive arena of platforms like TikTok, Facebook, and Instagram, leveraging viral content efficiently is crucial for maximizing earnings.

Firstly, you must understand that virality isn't just luck; it's also an opportunity. An opportunity that, if navigated wisely, can translate into a considerable income. The immediate aftermath of a viral hit is critical. While the digital world buzzes about your content, you should prepare to monetize this newfound attention. This could mean adding affiliate links to your posts, collaborating with brands for sponsored content, or directing traffic to a monetized YouTube channel or website.

Secondly, it's vital to engage with your audience in a timely manner. Acknowledge comments, answer questions, and be present. This helps to build a community around your content. With a loyal following, you create a platform for sustained earnings through community-driven platforms like Patreon or membership sites where your most dedicated fans can support you financially.

In the case of platforms like Instagram, turning a viral image or video into a sales opportunity can be as straightforward as utilizing the shopping feature or linking to merchandising partners' sites. The idea is to have these options in place before you go viral, so when your moment comes, you're ready to capitalize on it.

Furthermore, your viral content can be a goldmine for data collection. Learn from it. Understand the demographics, what caught their attention, and how it spread. This information is invaluable as it can inform your future content strategy, advertisements, and even product development to ensure they are tailored to what your audience wants.

Diversifying your content across various platforms is also key. If you're a hit on TikTok, why not repurpose that content for Instagram Reels or YouTube Shorts? Each platform has its way of monetizing content, and being present across these channels not only increases your visibility but also your potential revenue streams.

Having discussed diversification, let's talk about consistency. A viral video may give you a taste of fame, but consistency in producing high-quality content will help you to stay relevant. Regular posting will keep your audience engaged and can lead to continued viral successes. With constant engagement, the algorithms of these platforms are more likely to favor your content, making regular virality an achievable goal.

Remember that virality can often involve trending topics or timely content. Tie your subsequent content into these themes. Comprehensive understanding and capitalizing on trends are how viral content creators become viral brands. If a dance video brought you to fame's doorstep, think of accompanying merchandise, dance tutorials, or event appearances as potential revenue sources.

When your content does go viral, it's an excellent time to seek partnerships. Brands are always looking for successful content creators with a proven track record to endorse their products. Use the spotlight to negotiate deals and establish relationships that can offer more stable sources of income through sponsorships or endorsements.

Pivoting to brand work can also be incredibly lucrative post-virality. Use your viral content as a portfolio piece to showcase your influence and reach. This could open the door to being considered a thought leader or industry expert, leading to speaking engagements or consultancy roles, all of which can be monetized.

Next, consider the potential of licensing your content. If your viral moment has a unique aspect that is in demand, media outlets or other content creators might pay for the right to use it. In this digital age, licensing can become a recurring revenue for your viral media.

Another strategy is to use the momentum of virality to launch or promote your own products or services. If you're a fitness enthusiast who's gone viral, maybe it's time to introduce your line of workout programs or nutrition guides. This form of direct monetization has the potential to generate significant revenue.

Importantly, don't shy away from learning and adapting new social media skills to maintain the grip on your viral momentum. Online tools and courses can provide deep insights into SEO, content marketing, and social media ad campaigns enabling you to amplify and maintain your reach across various platforms.

Finally, always be sure to safeguard your content and understand the legalities surrounding social media earnings. Whether it's copyright laws or proper sponsor disclosure, staying compliant will protect your earnings and reputation in the long haul.

To wrap it up, leveraging viral content for maximum earnings isn't just about capitalizing on the moment. It's about seeing each viral success as a building block for your digital empire, crafting a strategy that encompasses engagement, monetization, and adaptation. Your viral content opens doors—choose wisely which ones to walk through, and always be ready to lead the charge towards your next viral hit and paycheck.

Chapter 7:
Lights, Camera, Cash:
Crafting Perfect Video Clips

Having delved into the nuances of virality and the power of social media platforms, it's time to fine-tune your approach to one of online content's most engaging formats: video. A captivating clip can catapult you into the spotlight and monetize your online presence like nothing else. In this pivotal chapter, we're setting the stage for you to create video content that not only grips your audience but also converts views into a tangible cash flow.

Video Content that Sells: Quality and Engagement

First things first: the hallmark of any engaging video is quality. This goes beyond high-definition imagery and crystal-clear sound—although those are certainly important. It's about a smooth blend of relevance, authenticity, and a touch of magic that captures the viewer's imagination. Consider what makes you stop scrolling and watch a video; the same elements will more than likely captivate your audience.

Your content should be a cocktail of entertainment and utility. Whether you're educating or exhilarating, the end goal is to hold your viewer's attention to the very last second. And let's not forget about engagement—a call to action is vital. Encourage comments, shares, and likes to foster a community around your content. Engagement not just boosts your visibility but also builds a rapport with your followers.

Tools of the Trade: Must-Have Gadgets and Software

No artisan can craft a masterpiece without the right tools, and the realm of video creation is no exception. There's a myriad of gadgets and software at your disposal, and selecting the right ones can elevate your content from good to great. From ring lights that cast a professional glow to editing software that adds that polished finish, your toolkit should empower your creative vision.

It's not necessary to invest a small fortune to start. Smartphones nowadays come equipped with cameras capable of shooting high-quality footage. Pair that with intuitive editing apps, and you've got a mini production studio right in the palm of your hand. As you grow, so can your array of gadgets and software, always aligned with the specific needs of your content and audience.

Remember, the allure of potential earnings through video content is strong, but your success hinges on the ability to produce clips that resonate and inspire. With each video you craft, consider the value it's delivering and the story it's telling. Combine your storytelling abilities with technical proficiency, and you'll not only captivate your audience but also unlock the door to monetization that video content so uniquely offers.

Explore the subsequent chapters for deeper insights into equipment selection, strategic content collaboration, and tactics to stimulate your followers into becoming customers. Every second of footage you capture is a stroke of your brush on the canvas of social media commerce. Make it count.

Video Content that Sells: Quality and Engagement

In the bustling world of social media, video content stands firmly at the forefront of engaging and capturing audiences. With platforms like TikTok, Instagram, and Facebook constantly evolving to prioritize visual storytelling, understanding the nexus of quality and engagement is pivotal for those wanting to turn their creative endeavors into lucrative streams of income.

Quality in video content isn't confined to high-definition visuals or the crystal-clear sound though these elements are undeniably essential. It's also an amalgamation of well-thought-out content, smooth editing, and an attention to detail that synchronizes with the heartbeat of your target audience. Remember, a sharp image can draw eyes, but it's the substance that will keep viewers watching, sharing, and coming back for more.

However, high-quality video doesn't mean you need the most expensive equipment. Your smartphone is a powerful tool capable of capturing stunning footage, given you understand the fundamentals of lighting and composition. Use natural light to your advantage and experiment with different angles to find the most flattering ones for your subject.

Equally important is sound quality. Viewers might forgive a less-than-perfect visual, but poor audio is often unforgivable. A basic microphone can vastly improve your clarity and reduce background noise, thus enhancing viewer experience. Investing in a good mic is investing in the professional feel of your content.

Once you've got the basics down, it's time to tackle engagement. The first few seconds of your video are crucial in hooking the viewer. Start with something that sparks curiosity or resonates with viewers' emotions. Ask yourself what your audience cares about, what makes them tick, and incorporate those triggers into your opening.

Storytelling is your power tool for engagement. Whether you're creating a how-to video, a product review, or just sharing a slice of life, there should be a clear narrative. Invite viewers on a journey — a journey they can relate to, learn from, or be entertained by. The narrative will be the thread that weaves through your video content, making it memorable and shareable.

Don't overlook the importance of pacing. Your video should move along briskly but not so fast that viewers can't follow. A well-paced video maintains viewers' attention by blending information with entertainment, without leaving them feeling overwhelmed or bored.

Engagement is also about interaction. Encourage viewers to engage by asking questions or inviting comments. Use calls-to-action (CTAs) to prompt responses, as these can lead to increased viewer participation and contribute to a sense of community around your content. This is where you start to see engagement convert to loyalty and, ultimately, to profit.

Consistency in your video content solidifies your brand. Posting regularly keeps you at the forefront of your viewers' minds and feeds the algorithms that favor active content creators. But consistency isn't just about frequency; it's about maintaining a level of quality and a style that your audience grows to know and love.

However, creating standout video content means understanding your platform's unique features and user behavior. For instance, what works on TikTok – usually quick, trend-driven content – might not have the same impact on Facebook, where in-depth exploration could be more appreciated. Tailor your video style and length appropriate to each platform for optimized engagement.

Don't shy away from analyzing your performance. Most platforms offer insights and analytics that can provide a window into what's working and what isn't. Track engagement metrics such as views, likes, shares, and comments to fine-tune your content strategy.

Let's also talk about authenticity — being genuine speaks volumes to viewers tired of traditional advertising and contrived content. Your realness can cut through the noise and foster a connection that's more likely to encourage viewer loyalty and conversion to sales. So, be yourself and let your unique personality shine through.

Lastly, engage with your community. Respond to comments, participate in discussions, and acknowledge your followers. This two-way interaction not only cements viewer relationships but also enhances your visibility and influence on the platform.

Mastering the art of video content is both a science and an art — requiring you to blend technical prowess with creative intuition. It's about fine-tuning each post for quality, optimizing it for platform-specific engagement, and always staying authentic to your brand. With these practices, you can turn simple video clips into powerful assets that drive traffic, build communities, and generate income right from your living room.

Your journey into crafting video content that sells is about continuous learning and adapting. Embrace feedback, innovate constantly, and don't be afraid to push the boundaries of your creativity. Your phone or computer screen isn't just a window to the world—it's a canvas, and with the right strokes, you can create something that not only captivates but also converts.

Tools of the Trade: Must-Have Gadgets and Software

In your journey to craft perfect video clips that captivate audiences and generate income on social media, you'll require an arsenal of tools that can take your content from good to phenomenal. This section is dedicated to equipping you with the must-have gadgets and software that will elevate your productions, streamline your workflow, and enhance your creative output.

A high-quality camera is non-negotiable if you're serious about video content creation. While your smartphone might suffice for starters, investing in a dedicated camera can dramatically improve the visual quality of your videos. Look for one with excellent video resolution, stability features, and the ability to perform well in various lighting conditions.

But let's not forget the importance of stellar audio. Poor sound quality can be a dealbreaker for viewers, no matter how stunning your visuals may be. A reliable microphone, be it a lavalier for on-the-go recording or a shotgun mic for directional capture, is essential for crisp, clear audio.

Lighting also plays a critical role in producing professional-looking videos. Softbox lights or LED ring lights provide a flattering and uniform light source, eliminating harsh shadows and highlighting your best features. Lighting can transform an ordinary video into a professional masterpiece.

Stabilization tools are a must for those action shots or on-the-move vlogs. A gimbal or a tripod will save the day, reducing shakiness and keeping your footage smooth as butter. Don't let a shaky hand be the downfall of your otherwise perfect clip.

Let's also talk software. For beginners, user-friendly editing programs are key. Tools like iMovie or Windows Video Editor can offer a gentle introduction to cutting, splicing, and refining your content. As you grow, software such as Adobe Premiere Pro or Final Cut Pro packs a punch with advanced features that can unleash your creative potential.

Graphics and animation can add pizazz to your videos, making them pop and catch the eye. Software like After Effects or simpler online tools like Canva, comes in handy to craft those visually attractive titles, transitions, and effects that can make your content stand out.

Audio editing software shouldn't be overlooked either. Audacity or Adobe Audition enables you to refine your sound, add music tracks, or tweak your voice to perfection. Remember, engaging content doesn't only please the eyes but also the ears.

Backing up your content is critical, and for that, reliable storage solutions are a must. External hard drives or cloud storage services ensure your precious footage is secure and accessible from anywhere, safeguarding against technical mishaps and data loss.

The role of streaming software is becoming increasingly prominent. If live content is your jam, OBS Studio or Streamlabs can be your best friends. They let you go live with ease, managing different sources and providing a platform to interact real-time with your audience.

With the rise of mobile content creation, don't ignore powerful mobile apps. Tools like InShot or FilmoraGo make video editing on-the-go a breeze, enabling creators to produce and upload content directly from their smartphones.

Monitoring and analytics software like Google Analytics or Social Blade will be pivotal to understanding what content resonates with your audience. You'll gain insights on performance metrics such as views, engagement rates, and audience demographics, allowing you to make data-driven decisions to grow your following and revenue.

Automation software, like Buffer or Hootsuite, helps you schedule posts across various platforms, maintain a consistent online presence, and manage your social media profiles in a more efficient way, giving you more time to focus on content creation.

Lastly, the importance of a fast and reliable computer can't be overstated. A machine with a solid processor and enough RAM will handle video editing tasks without hiccups. Don't let slow rendering times and crashes halt your creative process.

Armed with these essential gadgets and software, you're poised to create captivating, professional-quality video clips that can attract followers and open the doors to numerous monetization opportunities on social media. Remember that the quality of your content is crucial, but the quality of your tools can enhance your ability to produce it. Invest in your craft, embrace your creativity, and let these tools pave your way to online success.

Chapter 8:
Do-It-Yourself or Outsource?
The Solo Hustler's Dilemma

Navigating the world of social media requires a sharp mix of creativity, strategy, and practicality. Now, let's dive into a crucial question faced by countless digital entrepreneurs: should you take on the challenge of content creation solo, or is it time to hand the reins to a skilled professional? It's a pivotal decision that could pump vitality into your hustle or stall your growth if not approached with a discerning eye.

Let's crack into the essence of independent content creation. Think about the last viral video you encountered, or that immaculately curated Instagram feed that kept you scrolling for hours. Behind each of those digital wonders is a creator, someone who infused their personal touch into their content. Holding the title of 'content creator' means maintaining control over your vision and voice, thus ensuring that every piece you publish resonates with your brand identity.

However, DIY has its drawbacks. Knuckling down to create content demands time and often a diverse skill set that might not be your forte. From editing videos to perfecting that eye-catching graphic, these tasks can gobble up hours that could be channeled into strategizing and growing your brand's reach.

Here's where outsourcing sashays into the spotlight. There's an ocean of talented freelancers who can take your concept and turn it into reality, sometimes exceeding expectations. Hiring a graphic designer or a video editor can free you from the nitty-gritty, giving you the bandwidth to focus on the bigger picture.

But outsourcing isn't always a bed of roses. It can introduce complexities such as finding the right person for the job, clearly communicating your vision, and ensuring they deliver on time and on budget. Managing freelancers is an art in itself, one that requires you to hone your leadership and project management skills.

So, what's the call? To swing the pendulum in your favor, consider a couple of factors:

- **Scope and Scale**: Assess the scope of your content requirements against your available time and skills. If your goals outstretch your capacity, outsourcing parts of the process may be the way forward.
- **Cost vs. Investment**: Weigh the immediate costs of outsourcing against the potential return on investment. Will hiring help increase your content's quality and your revenue?

Remember, you don't have to choose exclusively between DIY and outsourcing. The beauty lies in the blend. Outsourcing certain tasks while maintaining a hands-on approach with others can craft a customized solution that's as unique as your social media hustle.

Your path to social media success isn't etched in stone; it's more like clay, moldable and ever-evolving. Whether you're gripping the tools of creation tightly in your own hands or passing them on to a craftsman in your field, the aim remains to build content that captures hearts and opens wallets.

Embrace the flexibility of your solo journey and know when to call in reinforcements. In the end, it's the wisdom to pivot between doing it all and delegating that marks the trail of a seasoned hustler.

Pros and Cons of Independent Content Creation

Diving headfirst into the world of social media can be a thrilling venture, and with it comes the decision every solo hustler faces: to create or to delegate? The allure of independent content creation is strong, as it offers a plethora of benefits that can be integral to your success online. Yet, as with any path chosen, there are also drawbacks that must be weighed.

One of the greatest advantages of creating content yourself is the control it affords you over your brand and your message. You have the autonomy to decide what to share, how to present it, and when it hits the digital airwaves. This direct line to your audience allows you to authentically express your vision, an invaluable component when building trust amongst your followers.

Moreover, when you're the mastermind behind your content, you reap the full financial rewards of your efforts. Instead of sharing profits with collaborators or outsourcing services, every dollar earned goes straight into your pocket. This benefit can't be overstated, especially when you're in the early stages of growing your social media empire.

Another aspect of going solo is the unparalleled opportunity for personal development. As you tackle video editing, graphic design, and content planning, you're gaining skills that will serve you today and tomorrow. This can be incredibly empowering and can lead to a sense of accomplishment that's hard to match.

However, independence comes with its share of cons. Content creation is a multi-faceted beast, and it demands a significant investment of time. Crafting those perfect posts, engaging with followers, and keeping up with social media trends is a full-time job in itself. Time is one of your most valuable assets and should be spent wisely.

Additionally, being a jack-of-all-trades means you might not be able to master any single aspect of content creation to a professional level. This is where the quality of your work may suffer. Content that looks amateurish can detract from your brand's credibility and may make it difficult to compete with those who have professional help.

Furthermore, the pressure of constantly producing new, compelling content can be overwhelming. Creator burnout is very real, presenting not only a barrier to consistent posting but also a risk to your well-being. When you're responsible for every facet of content creation, the balance between work and life can blur.

Focusing only on content creation might also mean missing out on networking opportunities and strategic partnerships. An outsourced creator or team can free you up to attend events, engage in collaborations, or explore new platforms, growing your reach and influence.

Imagine, too, the technical challenges that inevitably arise. When hardware fails or software bewilders, you are your own IT department. For those less technically inclined, such problems can result in delayed postings or diminished content quality, which in turn, can impact engagement and earnings.

It's also key to note the limitations on scalability. As one person, your capacity to create and distribute content has a ceiling. If you're handling everything independently, reaching beyond that ceiling would be difficult, potentially capping your growth and income potential.

On the flip side, the agility of solo content creation has its merits. You're able to pivot quickly, reacting to trends or audience feedback in real time -- a flexibility that might be lost when more parties are involved. In an ever-changing digital landscape, this can be a key to staying relevant.

That said, the isolation that comes with the territory can be daunting. Without collaborators, you may miss out on the creative synergy that comes from shared ideas and expertise. Often, two (or more) minds are better than one, particularly when it comes to brainstorming fresh, groundbreaking content.

Let's not overlook the educational aspect. By creating content yourself, you're forced to stay at the cutting edge of social media trends, tools, and tactics. This can make you a stronger, more informed marketer and creator — an impressive feat if you can manage the learning curve.

However, when every decision, from concept to post-production, rests on you, the likelihood of bias and blind spots increases. An outside perspective can offer insights into your content that you may not have considered, potentially steering you away from mistakes or opening up new avenues for growth.

In conclusion, independent content creation can be a goldmine for those who crave control, personal growth, and full financial gains. But, it's a path lined with potential pitfalls including time constraints, quality concerns, burnout, and limited scalability. Weigh these pros and cons carefully, knowing that your choice will shape your social media journey and ultimately, your success.

When to Consider Outsourcing

In the bustling world of social media money-making, time is often your most restricted commodity. As you sail through the realms of Facebook, Instagram, TikTok, and the enigmatic Threads, the value of an hour can be the difference between opportunity seized and opportunity missed. Here, the lone hustler stands at the crossroads: **Do-It-Yourself** or **Outsource**? You may excel in crafting sensational posts and videos that captivate hearts and minds, but even the most skilled content creators reach a point where scaling up demands external assistance.

Consider outsourcing when you notice that routine tasks consume substantial chunks of your creative time. If you find the hours spent on photo editing, comment moderation, or administrative work overtaking the time devoted to strategy and content creation, it's time to assess the balance. Recognizing the need for help isn't a sign of weakness, but a strategic move toward sustainable growth and sharpened focus.

Furthermore, explore the prospects of outsourcing when specialized skills are required. Let's say video editing isn't your forte, but it's essential for your Instagram and TikTok ventures. Delegating this task to a professional can significantly amplify your content's impact. In another vein, perhaps understanding the intricate algorithms and data analytics of these platforms isn't your cup of tea. Hiring an expert can provide insights that refine your approach, ensuring you stay ahead of the ever-changing viral trends.

Outsourcing is equally pivotal when scaling operations. Diving into the whirlwind of social media success, one quickly learns that maintaining consistency is key. But with success comes demand—more content, more engagement, more growth. This is a glorious turning point, where entrenching allies, both in freelancing and professional services, can help your cause.

Lastly, consider your wellbeing. The relentless pace of managing a social media presence can take a toll. Outsourcing can give you the breather needed to sustain your passion and prevent burnout. Balancing life and the digital hustle is no easy feat, and sometimes allowing others to share the load can rejuvenate your spirits and give you the space to generate fresh, invigorating ideas.

In essence, outsourcing should be viewed as a critical component in the architecture of your online empire—a strategic decision that can catapult your solo endeavors into a symphony of collaborative success. As you ponder over this pivotal step, remember that the goal is not merely to free up time, but to elevate the quality and reach of your content to levels that resonate even louder across the digital landscape.

Finding and Managing Freelancers

In the bustling cosmos of social media, agility and creativity are your stalwarts. While you have learned the rudiments of building your empire online, there's a fundamental turning point you'll reach—the junction where you ponder whether to maintain your do-it-yourself ethos or to expand your horizons through delegation. Outsourcing to freelancers can inject your projects with fresh ideas, specialized skills, and allow you the freedom to focus on growth strategies for your brand. If your fingers are hovering over the keyboard, ready to dive into this untapped reservoir of talent, let's guide you through the process of finding and managing freelancers effectively.

When you're contemplating outsourcing, consider the tasks that consume a sizable chunk of your time but are not necessarily within your wheelhouse. Be it graphic design, content writing, or video editing, freelancers with expertise in these domains can elevate the quality of your content, which is paramount in the visually driven platforms of Instagram and TikTok. The key is to identify the tasks that, when handed to pros, can amplify your presence and profitability.

The search for the ideal freelancer begins with a quest—a quest for someone who doesn't merely complete tasks but does so aligning with your brand's spirit and voice. Platforms like Upwork, Fiverr, and Freelancer are overflowing with skilled individuals ready to collaborate. Each platform comes with its own set of strengths, be it scope, budget flexibility, or niche skills. It's essential to craft a comprehensive job description that delineates your expectations, standards, and vision to attract proposals that resonate with your brand's needs.

Once you've cast your net and the applications start flooding in, start the vetting process. Pay keen attention to their portfolios, harnessing your keen eye for content that has been thriving on your social media channels. The freelancers' past work should speak to you – it should tell you that they can embody the essence of your brand, that they understand the dynamic nature of social media and that they can consistently deliver high-quality work.

Conducting interviews may seem a touch formal in the digital age, but they're indispensable. Video calls or even voice interviews can unveil a freelancer's communication skills and responsiveness—traits crucial for seamless collaboration. This is a synergy you're seeking and a rapport that could make or break the quality of your content.

Negotiating rates is a step that cannot be sidestepped. Remember that while it's tempting to veer towards the lowest bidder to maximize profit, what matters most is value. It's a balancing act of respecting the freelancer's worth and ensuring that you're getting a return on investment that makes sense for your business. Striking this balance is an art—master it.

Onboarding is the phase where expectations meet reality. Here, provide clear guidelines, style references, and articulate your brand's voice. It's about paving a path for the freelancer to walk on, a path that leads directly to the goals you've set. Familiarize them with the trends of your particular social media niche, the nuances of your audience, and the general ethos of your brand narrative.

Project management tools can become your best ally in this endeavor. Platforms like Trello, Asana, or Notion can help keep tasks organized, priorities in check, and deadlines sacred. They can also foster a transparent working relationship, with clear benchmarks and easy tracking of progress.

Milestones are the buoys that guide the ship of your collaboration. Define clear outcomes and check-in points to align both your freelancer's contributions with your timeline and quality expectations. Celebrate the completions and dissect the complications—the project should be dynamic and adapt with each lesson learned.

Communication is the bridge between confusion and clarity. Keep lines open, feedback constructive, and compliments generous. Thrive on regular updates, but avoid micromanagement. You are cultivating a professional relationship built on mutual respect and understanding, not just churning out assignments.

As projects come to completion, it's vital to review the work meticulously. Analyze the impact of each piece of content. Has your engagement surged? Are your followers beginning to recognize a pattern of quality that wasn't there before? This feedback loop is what will help you sustain long-term relationships with freelancers who truly add value to your social media presence.

Payment processes should be prompt and transparent. Use established systems like PayPal, Stripe, or the platform's payment service to maintain trust. A freelancer who feels appreciated and valued is more likely to deliver consistently high-quality work and go the extra mile for your brand.

Now, let's address the not-so-pleasant part: There will be times when a freelancer doesn't work out. They might miss deadlines, deliver subpar quality, or simply not gel with your brand. When such occasions arise, handle them with professionalism. Provide clear and honest feedback, sever ties if needed respectfully, but keep the door open for potential future collaboration under different circumstances.

Maintaining a network of freelancers can become a talent pool you can dip into as needed. Cultivate these relationships, because in the nimble world of social media, having a reliable Rolodex of creative individuals can be the key that unlocks new doors of opportunity for your brand.

With this arsenal of strategies and considerations in hand, you are now well-equipped to navigate the thriving freelancing landscape. Remember, your brand isn't just what you post; it's also about the team behind the content. Choose wisely, manage wisely, and watch as your digital hustle scales new heights and your streams of income diversify, bolstered by the collaboration with talents who can take your content from good to extraordinary.

Chapter 9:
Work Smarter, Not Harder: Automation and Tools

As we dive into Chapter 9, let's pivot to a vital aspect of scaling up your online money-making ventures: the art of working smarter, not harder. In this digital era, automation and innovative tools are your ultimate allies, empowering you to maximize efficiency while minimizing unnecessary toil. Whether you're operating from a state-of-the-art home office or simply your smartphone, embracing technology will catapult your productivity to unprecedented heights.

Essential Social Media Tools for Efficiency

Imagine for a moment that your online presence is a garden. Without the proper tools, you'd be hand-picking weeds and watering each plant one by one—a surefire path to exhaustion. The digital landscape is much the same. Thankfully, a range of tools exists to streamline your social media workflow. From content calendars like Trello to analytics platforms such as Google Analytics, these tools enable you to plan, execute, and measure your online success with remarkable precision.

However, the journey doesn't stop there. Cutting-edge solutions such as Buffer and Hootsuite permit you to schedule posts across multiple platforms, all from one dashboard. That's right—you can coordinate your TikTok posts, Instagram stories, and Facebook updates seamlessly, allowing for a cohesive brand narrative that engages followers while you sleep. And let's not forget graphic design tools like Canva, which simplify the creation of eye-catching visuals, making sure your posts stand out in a crowded digital universe.

Automating Your Way to Passive Income

Now, let's tap into automation, the silent powerhouse of passive income. In your journey to financial freedom, think of automation as your autopilot, navigating through the intricacies of cyberspace while you focus on the big picture.

Email marketing services, such as Mailchimp or ConvertKit, are quintessential for automating your outreach, building an engaged community around your brand without the grind of manual messaging. Chatbots can manage customer service inquiries on your platform of choice, keeping the conversation lively and your audience attended to 24/7.

Affiliate marketing programs can be set to run in the background of your content, generating revenue with each click and conversion. And let's not overlook the potential of automated ad management systems that optimize your campaigns on the fly, ensuring a profitable return on investment.

Equipping yourself with these tools and automation strategies does more than save time—it opens the door to new opportunities. You can now explore collaborations, expand your creative horizons, or even take a well-deserved break without disrupting the flow of income.

In conclusion, Chapter 9 isn't just about introducing handy tools and automation hacks. It's about transforming your approach to online money-making, by investing in systems that work tirelessly behind the scenes. Embrace the smart path forward, and watch as your digital empire thrives, supported by foundations of innovation and efficiency.

Now, as we prepare to enter Chapter 10, and you're well-armed with the knowledge of automation, it's time to zero in on building a formidable and authentic social media brand—a brand that resonates with your audience and stands the test of time.

Essential Social Media Tools for Efficiency

In the quest to monetize social media, mastering the art of efficiency plays a critical role. As we dive into the myriad of tools designed to streamline your social media endeavors, remember that the right set of tools can elevate your online presence and income potential exponentially.

When considering the vast social media landscape, you need a content scheduler at your disposal. Tools like Buffer, Hootsuite, or Later are not just time-savers; they're lifelines in keeping a consistent posting schedule across platforms. By batching content and scheduling it in advance, you're free to focus on crafting impactful posts rather than being weighed down by the daily grind of manual posting.

Graphics and visual content are essential, and apps like Canva or Adobe Spark become invaluable. With their user-friendly interfaces, these tools enable you to create professional-looking images or graphics without a steep learning curve or a hefty investment into expensive design software.

Don't overlook the power of analytics. Platforms such as Sprout Social, or the built-in insights provided by Instagram and Facebook, empower you with data-driven decisions. Understanding what content resonates with your audience means you can tailor your strategy for increased engagement and income potential.

Engagement doesn't have to be a 24/7 job. Engagement tools like SocialBee or ManageFlitter help you stay connected with your followers without being chained to your device. Automating likes, follows, and even personalized messages can keep your community thriving while you strategize the bigger picture.

Email marketing remains a potent tool, and integrating services like Mailchimp or ConvertKit bridges the gap between social media and email lists. Capturing leads from your social media audience enables you to reach out to them directly, bypassing ever-changing algorithms.

A frequent pain point for content creators is keeping up with all the comments and messages. Tools like AgoraPulse or Sprout Social aggregate messages from multiple platforms into a single inbox, facilitating swift and organized responses.

Short-form video content is all the rage, and with TikTok leading the pack, tools like InShot or Splice are essential for editing on the fly. Crisp, engaging, and professional-looking videos can be made in minutes, allowing you to capitalize on trends as they happen.

For those delving into livestreaming, software like Streamyard or OBS Studio streamlines the process, making it accessible and high-quality. Engaging with your audience in real-time increases authenticity and, by extension, loyalty and the likelihood of monetization.

Hashtag research tools such as HashtagsForLikes or Keyword Tool can greatly enhance your content's discoverability. Strategic hashtag use is critical in expanding your content's reach, especially when you're aiming to tap into new audiences.

Collaborations and sponsorships are key in monetizing social presence, and platforms like Upfluence or AspireIQ connect you with brands that align with your niche. These make the process of securing partnerships far more efficient, letting you focus on creating content that both your audience and potential sponsors will love.

Lastly, let's not forget about project management tools such as Trello, Asana, or Monday.com. When your social media activities turn into a full-scale operation, coordination becomes crucial. These tools help you keep all your strategies, ideas, and processes neatly organized and on track.

Each of these tools serves to enhance not only your efficiency but also the quality of your work. By using them wisely, you can streamline operations, devote more energy to creative endeavors, and, most importantly, transform your social media into a profitable enterprise.

Investing in these tools isn't just about saving time; it's about making each moment count twice as much. As your social media business grows, your tools and systems should evolve with it. Keep abreast of new developments, and be ready to adapt your toolkit to sustain and enhance your online success.

Remember, while these tools are powerful, they are but extensions of your vision and hard work. They enable you, but at the heart, your content is king, and engaging with your audience is the kingdom. Employ these essentials with care and watch as your social media platforms transform into sources of substantial, sustainable income.

Automating Your Way to Passive Income

In an era where time is a precious commodity, finding efficient methods to create wealth is paramount. Those looking to maximize their earnings from social media must harness technology to their advantage. This is where automation enters the picture, transforming your online hustle into a well-oiled passive income machine.

Imagine your social media presence working for you, even while you sleep. With automation tools, it's more than possible—it's a game changer. These tools can take repetitive tasks off your hands, from posting content to engaging with followers. This frees up time for you to focus on crafting a more impactful online presence—or simply to enjoy life away from the screen.

To start the automation journey, investigate scheduling software specifically designed for social media platforms. Whether it's TikTok, Facebook, Instagram, or Threads, there's a solution tailored to streamline your postings. Plan your content calendar in advance, and let these tools post at the optimal times for engagement, keeping your profile active and consistent without constant manual input.

Next up are analytics tools, which play a crucial part in understanding what content resonates with your audience. They can automatically track performance metrics and provide insights that will shape your future content strategy. Use this data to identify trends and patterns, which can be capitalized on to drive more traffic to your profiles, thus increasing potential revenue.

Email marketing automation is another puzzle piece that shouldn't be ignored. By building an email list through your social media channels, you can nurture and convert followers into loyal customers. Automation services can send personalized, timely emails based on user behavior, leading to higher conversion rates and sustained income.

Chatbots are another innovative solution for automating engagement. A well-programed chatbot can interact with your audience, answer frequently asked questions, and even guide them towards purchases, leaving you more time to work on the bigger picture.

Moreover, affiliate marketing can be largely automated. If you've built an audience that trusts your recommendations, affiliate links can be subtly woven into your automated content, generating revenue as followers make purchases based on your influence.

And let's not forget the power of automating the monetization process itself. Platforms like Facebook and Instagram offer tools that can detect when your content meets the criteria for monetization and enable ads without you lifting a finger.

Adopting these automation strategies, however, should be done carefully. Authenticity is the bedrock of social media success; too much automation can come off as impersonal and damage that trust.

Striking the right balance between automated and personal touch is critical in maintaining your brand's authenticity.

It's also important to remember that setup does take time and patience. Learning to use these tools effectively might feel overwhelming at first, but once they're in motion, the time investment pays off immensely.

As you dive deeper into automation, you may want to explore advanced options like cross-platform integration tools. These are designed to synchronize your profiles across different social media, ensuring your brand message is cohesive and saving you from managing each platform individually.

Furthermore, consider automating aspects of your content creation. Various programs can generate basic content based on set parameters, which can then be tweaked and personalized by you. This paves the way for a consistent stream of content, a cornerstone of sustained social media engagement.

Automation also extends beyond content to the administrative side of social media. Invoicing, reporting, and tracking payments can all be streamlined. Tools like these reduce the mundanity of day-to-day operations, letting you focus on the big picture—scaling your income sources.

The beauty of all these tools is that they allow for more strategic planning. With the day-to-day taken care of, you can brainstorm innovative ways to engage your audience, collaborate with brands, and maybe even start your own product lines—all significant steps towards increasing your passive income.

Last but not least, don't forget to periodically check on the health of your automation systems. Like any technology, they require maintenance. By ensuring they function correctly, you'll prevent potential hiccups that could interrupt your earning flow.

Automation is not about replacing the human element; it's about amplifying it. By eliminating the repetitive tasks, you empower yourself to use your time creatively and strategically. Fully embracing automation on social media is an investment that, when done right, will pay dividends, propelling you towards the financial autonomy everyone desires.

Chapter 10:
Building Your Social Media Brand

In the bustling digital marketplace, carving out a niche for yourself is as crucial as having a valuable product or service to offer. Your social media brand is your identity - the distinct personality that becomes synonymous with your online presence. By now, you've learned about different platforms and strategies to monetize them. But without a strong, recognizable brand, even the most strategic efforts can fall flat. Let's explore how to craft a social media brand that resonates with audiences and turns engagement into income. Remember, it's not just about what you're selling, but the story you're telling.

Defining Your Online Persona

Think of your favorite social media influencer or business. What comes to mind? Chances are, it's not just a product, but a feeling, an attitude, and a style that's distinctly theirs. That's branding at its best. As you build your social media brand, start by asking yourself, "*Who am I in the digital world?*" This persona should align with your values but also appeal to your target demographic. Finessing your online presence isn't about donning a facade; it's about amplifying certain facets of your personality that resonate most with your audience.

Consider your tone, style, and the topics you engage with. Will you be the authoritative voice in your field, the ever-curious learner, or the casual friend sharing tips over coffee? The persona you adopt can open the door to a community of like-minded individuals who trust your voice among the cacophony of the internet.

Trust and Authenticity: The Currencies of Social Media

Now, let's talk currency. Not the greenbacks you're aiming to earn, but the social currency that is trust and authenticity. These are the gold standards of the social media world. In an age where consumers are besieged by ads and sponsored content, transparency isn't just appreciated—it's expected. Building trust with your following is a non-negotiable foundation of a successful online brand.

Authenticity breathes life into your brand. Share your successes, sure, but also your struggles. Let your audience behind the scenes; show them the real, unpolished journey. Being authentic fosters a connection that transcends mere transactions. When your audience feels like they know the real you, they're more likely to stick around—and more inclined to support what you're selling.

Be consistent in your messaging, engage genuinely, and deliver value always. Each post should contribute to the narrative you're weaving. When potential followers stumble upon your content for the first time, they should immediately grasp who you are and what you stand for.

Taking these principles to heart and applying them to your digital endeavors will put you on the path to creating a brand that not only stands out but also stands the test of time. Invest in your social media brand, and watch as it repays you with loyalty, engagement, and yes, a healthier bottom line. With an authentic and trusted brand, you become not just a player in the digital market, but a destination.

Build your brand with the confidence that it's the unique story only you can tell. The world is waiting to hear it. And with the groundwork laid out in the preceding chapters, you're more than ready to deliver. Make your next move with intention, purpose, and a dash of flair. Your brand isn't just a logo or a color scheme; it's the heart and soul of your online identity.

With a strong social media brand, the trust you've invested in will become the currency that opens unlimited doors for your online journey. The road to success is paved with the connections you make along the way—and those connections start with a brand that authentically represents you.

Defining Your Online Persona

Building a compelling online presence requires you to craft a persona that resonates with your audience while reflecting your genuine self. Your online persona is the character you present to the cyber world—it's a blend of your personal interests, professional expertise, and the unique quirks that make you, well, you. It serves as the foundation for every tweet, every Instagram photo, and every TikTok video you create.

When embarking on this journey, consider your online persona to be your brand ambassador, greeting and engaging with followers 24/7. This is whom people will come to know, to love, to trust, and to buy from. It's not something to be taken lightly. The authenticity of your persona is what will differentiate you from the sea of sameness on social media.

Start by pinpointing what interests you most. Are you a fashion enthusiast, a tech whiz, or a health guru? Your passions will fuel your content and help attract a like-minded audience. But passion alone isn't enough. You need to add in your unique perspective or skill set—this is what will make you stand out. Your perspective is your secret sauce, your unique selling proposition, ensuring that your voice is heard amidst the noise.

Think also about the characteristics and values that you want to be associated with. Do you want to be seen as knowledgeable and insightful, or witty and entertaining? Your tone and the way you interact with your audience should consistently reflect these attributes.

It's important not to confuse creating a persona with inventing a fake identity. The most successful online personas are rooted in authenticity. Make sure that you're not projecting an image that is completely at odds with who you are in real life. Incongruence can be easily spotted and may lead to a loss of trust—and followers.

Your online persona should be tailored to the platform you're using. Each social media platform has its own culture and language. The polished images and curated feeds that work on Instagram may not translate well to TikTok's raw and real vibe. You'll need to adapt your persona to fit the norms of each platform while still maintaining a consistent identity.

Consistency is key. Once you've defined your persona, stick with it across all platforms. This doesn't mean all your content needs to be the same—different platforms excite different aspects of your persona—but the underlying principles, your values, and your style should be cohesive. Whether it's a tweet, a Facebook post, or a TikTok video, your audience should instantly recognize it's you.

Visual branding is a part of this equation too. Choose colors, logos, and fonts that represent your brand's personality and use them consistently. When someone sees your content, your visual branding should work seamlessly with your online persona to leave a memorable impression.

Engage with your followers as your true self. Your online persona isn't a monologue—it's a dialogue with your audience. Engage with your followers by responding to comments, asking for their opinions, and showing appreciation. This humanizes your brand and makes it more relatable.

Balance professionalism with personality. Even if you're using social media for business, don't be afraid to show some personal aspects. People connect with people, not faceless brands. Sharing snippets of your personal life or behind-the-scenes content can make your brand more approachable.

When sharing personal content, however, set boundaries. Decide early on what aspects of your personal life are off-limits and stick to these decisions. Boundaries protect your privacy and ensure you're comfortable with the persona you project online.

Be prepared to evolve. Just as we evolve as individuals, your online persona can—and should—develop over time. As your interests expand and you gain more insight into what your audience enjoys, don't be afraid to refine your persona. Just ensure that these changes are gradual and don't alienate your audience.

Finally, analyze and iterate. Use the built-in analytics tools on social platforms to study how your audience engages with different aspects of your persona. What content do they love? What drives the most interaction? These insights allow you to hone in on what works best, helping you to grow your brand strategically.

Creating and defining your online persona is a nuanced and ongoing process. It's the avatar through which you'll communicate with the world, and it forms the bedrock of your social media brand. It determines the kind of audience you attract, the partnerships you form, and the opportunities that come your way. Handle it with care, thought, and above all, an unyielding commitment to authenticity, and watch as you transform your digital hustle into a thriving, profitable brand.

With your online persona well-defined and radiating confidence, the next chapter will dive into the currencies of social media—trust and authenticity. These elements are critical as they dictate your engagement, reputation, and ultimately, your ability to monetize your presence. Your persona is set, now it's time to build a relationship with your audience that's as real as it gets, even in the virtual world.

Trust and Authenticity: The Currencies of Social Media

In the realm of social media, trust and authenticity aren't just good-to-haves, they're the very currencies that determine your brand's value. Building your social media brand requires more than just a consistent posting schedule and engaging content; you must cultivate a reputation steeped in trustworthiness and authenticity.

Diving deeper, trust is the bedrock of any relationship, and that includes the digital connections you foster with your audience. When followers trust you, they're more inclined to engage with your content, share your posts, and support your monetization efforts. It's a simple equation: trust leads to loyalty, and loyalty leads to revenue.

But how do you build trust? Transparency is key. Show your followers the person behind the posts, the fails along with the wins, and the reality behind the polished images. This doesn't mean exposing every aspect of your life but rather letting people in on your journey, the process, and the hard work that goes into your success.

Authenticity is your ally here. It's about being genuine in your interactions, staying true to your values, and maintaining a consistent voice across all platforms. People can spot insincerity from a mile away, especially in the digital landscape where authenticity stands out. It's about keeping it real, even when it feels risky.

Case in point: think about the influencers who admit when they've been sponsored to talk about a product. Their honesty not only complies with legal requirements but also builds trust. The audience doesn't feel deceived, and this transparency translates to a tighter bond between creator and follower.

Furthermore, a sense of authenticity inspires. It's compelling to watch someone who is passionate about their niche, who believes in their message, and who isn't swayed by the latest trends unless they align with their brand. Authenticity isn't just about staying in your lane; it's about owning it, knowing it, and becoming the go-to in your field.

But remember, building trust and authenticity isn't an overnight process. It's a continual investment of time and energy. With each post, comment, and message, you have the opportunity to reinforce these values. And sometimes, it means making tough choices for the integrity of your brand.

Take, for example, turning down lucrative deals that don't fit your brand's message or sacrificing short-term gains for long-term credibility. It's a fine balance, striking the right chords of enterprise and integrity, where your audience knows that if you've shared something, you stand behind it 100%.

Engagement is another crucial component. When you're responsive to your community, you're reinforcing that trust. It's not just about replying to comments or messages, but engaging in meaningful conversations and showing that you value their input. This two-way interaction isn't just good manners; it's smart business.

Also, never underestimate the power of storytelling. Sharing your experiences, the hurdles you've overcome, and the milestones you've hit makes you relatable. People don't just buy products; they buy into stories and the people behind them. A great narrative can elevate your brand from a business to a movement.

And what about authenticity in the face of criticism? It's simple: take it gracefully. Every response to critique is a chance to strengthen trust. Sometimes that means standing your ground, other times it means acknowledging a mistake. Either way, it's another deposit in the trust bank of your audience.

Bear in mind, your digital footprint is long-lasting, and inconsistencies are called out quickly. So align your online persona with who you are and what you stand for. This congruence between your virtual self and your real-world self will resonate with followers. They're looking for something genuine, and that's a torch you have to carry every day.

Utilizing testimonials and user-generated content can foster trust too. Seeing others endorse your brand carries weight, lending credibility and real-world proof that what you're offering or representing is worth their time and money.

This can't be emphasized enough: don't get lost in vanity metrics. It's better to have a smaller, engaged following that trusts you than millions of followers who don't connect with your brand. These connections lead to conversions and are central to monetizing your social media platforms.

To conclude, trust and authenticity are currencies that you can't afford to neglect. They dictate the sustainability and growth of your social media brand. Nourish them, protect them, and watch them return the investment tenfold. Your brand's authenticity and the trust you cultivate are gateways to not just surviving in the competitive world of social media, but thriving in it.

Chapter 11:
The Legal Side of Social Media Earnings

As you venture further into the realm of social media earnings, there's a critical dimension that's essential to your success, and it's not just about understanding algorithms and engagement—it's about grasping the legalities that underpin your online activities. Acknowledging the legal side isn't just about playing it safe; it's about fortifying your business, preserving your creative assets, and ensuring that your revenue streams stay open and flowing.

Understanding Copyrights, Sponsorships and Disclosures

Entering the digital fray, where content is king, you must understand the rules of copyright. When creating and sharing content, ensure it's either original, licensed or falls within fair use. It's not just a matter of respect—it's about avoiding costly legal disputes that could cripple your social media success.

Sponsorships are a golden ticket on this journey, but with great deals come great responsibilities. Transparency is key. Always reveal the nature of your partnerships with brands. It's not just good ethics; it's a requirement enforced by the Federal Trade Commission. Your audience values honesty, and so do the legal authorities.

Protecting Yourself and Your Profits Online

As your social media presence blossoms and your profits increase, protecting your assets becomes imperative. Start thinking about forming a legal entity for your business such as an LLC. It's a shield for your personal assets and a message that you're serious about your business.

Moreover, don't shy away from legal advice. A consultation with an intellectual property attorney can save you from pitfalls you might not even see coming. Do your due diligence on contracts and agreements. While it's tempting to ride the wave of every opportunity, a careful review can be the difference between a beneficial collaboration and a regrettable mistake.

Always remember, the bridge between your online endeavors and sustained profitability is paved with legal wisdom. It's not enough to make money; you must know how to keep it. Invest in your legal knowledge as you do in your content and watch your digital empire stand the test of time.

With every post, every deal, and every connection, carry with you the awareness that these pixels and platforms are more than tools—they are the foundations of a business that demands legal mindfulness. Innovate, create, and share, but above all, be legally savvy so that what you build today endures and thrives tomorrow.

Understanding Copyrights, Sponsorships and Disclosures

When venturing into the bustling world of social media earnings, it's imperative to grasp the gravity of legal concepts like copyrights, sponsorships, and disclosures. Far from being an arid terrain of legalese, these concepts are the bedrock upon which you can solidify your online business and protect your creative investments.

Copyrights are a form of protection provided by the laws of the United States to the authors of "original works of authorship," including literary, dramatic, musical, artistic, and certain other intellectual works. If you're creating content, whether it's blogs, videos or photos for social media, you're creating copyrightable material. Understanding what is protected under copyright law, what isn't, and how to ensure that your work respects the rights of others is crucial.

Let's dive into sponsorships. The hunger for authentic content has led brands to team up with influencers and content creators. Such partnerships can be immensely profitable, but they're laden with responsibility. Sponsorships demand transparency. When you endorse a product, your audience must know whether you're paid for the promotion. The Federal Trade Commission (FTC) requires clear disclosures so consumers can distinguish between organic endorsements and sponsored content.

Disclosures aren't just legal necessities; they're trust-building tools. They detail your relationships with brands and if you've received any compensation for a piece of content. The key is clarity – your disclosures should be conspicuous and understandable. A hidden or confusing disclosure can erode trust with your audience and bring unwelcome attention from regulatory bodies.

Now, how do you navigate these waters? First, when you use music, imagery, or video clips that you didn't create, make sure you have the right to use them. This can be through licenses or because the work is in the public domain or under Creative Commons. Don't assume that just because something is online that it's free to use. That's a fast track to copyright infringement accusations.

In sponsorships, start by choosing brands that align with your values and audience to maintain authenticity. When you do promote, use clear language like "Sponsored by" or "Paid partnership with" and ensure this disclosure is easily seen or heard. On video content, an on-screen graphic or an upfront verbal acknowledgment works well.

Creating your own content outrightly circumvents a lot of copyright issues and places you as the rightful owner. However, it's also wise to be clued into how copyright law protects you from having your work used without permission. You might also dive into trademarks to safeguard your personal brand or catchphrases that become synonymous with your online persona.

Be mindful that while US copyright laws are vital, social media is global. Other countries have their own laws and regulations, which can come into play if your content crosses borders. This aspect emphasizes the importance of a versatile strategy that adheres to international standards when necessary.

Moreover, consider the nuances of "fair use" – a legal doctrine that permits limited use of copyrighted material without requiring permission from the rights holders. This includes uses such as commentary, criticism, news reporting, and scholarly research. Knowing how and when fair use applies is a skill that could serve you well, especially as a content creator looking to comment on or review others' work.

The beauty of disclosures is that they don't have to be a creativity stifler; rather, they can be woven into your content naturally and transparently. Infuse them into your narrative or visuals in a way that's both artistic and responsible. Make it part of your brand's story – your commitment to honesty.

Keep in mind, too, that as your platform grows, so does the scrutiny. It isn't just about following the rules now but also about anticipating the ethical standards of tomorrow. As influencers and content creators are increasingly seen as role models, their actions under the microscope can set examples for millions.

Empower yourself with knowledge about image rights and the permissible use of other's content. There are stock image websites, music libraries offering royalty-free tracks, and platforms to buy rights to use other creators' content. These sources can furnish your work without stepping on legal toes.

What if you falter? If you happen to infringe a copyright or miss a disclosure, it's not the end of the road. Rectify the issue promptly, learn from the misstep, and establish a more vigilant process for the future. The digital sphere is rather forgiving, provided you act with integrity and a willingness to correct course.

Remember, at the heart of copyrights, sponsorships, and disclosures is the promotion of fair play and respect within the online ecosystem. They ensure that creators get due credit and audiences are not misled. You're not just safeguarding your business but also nurturing the trust that is so vital in the online community.

Lastly, it can't be stressed enough – when in doubt, seek legal counsel. A short consultation with an intellectual property attorney can save you from a mountain of trouble down the line. Equipped with the right knowledge and strategies, you can navigate the legal landscape of social media earnings with confidence and continue to thrive online.

As we forge ahead, it's clear that understanding the legalities of copyrights, sponsorships, and disclosures is more than mere compliance – it's an investment in your brand's longevity and integrity. With this knowledge securely under your belt, you're well on your way to monetizing your presence across the vast realms of social media – responsibly and profitably.

Protecting Yourself and Your Profits Online

As you venture further into the realm of social media earnings, it's vital to recognize that while the digital space offers an abundance of opportunities, it's also rife with potential pitfalls. Protecting both yourself and your profits is not merely wise—it's an absolute necessity for sustained success. In this chapter, we delve into the safeguards you need to put in place to ensure your online endeavors are secure and profitable for years to come.

Firstly, intellectual property rights are the linchpin of creative online content. Understand and respect copyright laws—it's imperative to protect your own creative assets as you would guard a precious treasure. It may seem like a labyrinth of legalese, but one way to keep your work under your control is to trademark your brand and copyright your original content. When you've poured your heart and your mind into an original piece, the last thing you want is someone else reaping the rewards.

Next, consider the aspect of online security. You'll be handling sensitive information, not just yours but that of your subscribers or customers as well. Investing in robust cybersecurity can't be overstated. Be it sophisticated passwords, two-factor authentication, or encrypted communications, making sure that your digital domain is fortified against cyber threats is a non-negotiable aspect of online business.

Furthermore, when engaging in brand partnerships and sponsorships, it is crucial to vet every opportunity thoroughly. Transparency with your audience about sponsored content is not only a legal requirement but also helps maintain your reputation. Craft clear, genuine endorsements and always include proper disclosures. The Federal Trade Commission (FTC) has stringent guidelines pertaining to this, and you wouldn't want your hard-earned credibility tarnished by legal missteps.

Also, have contracts in place when collaborating with other creatives or outsourcing. In the online world, a well-structured contract is like a lifejacket in choppy waters—it's there to keep you afloat should disputes arise. It's the hallmark of professionalism and ensures that expectations and compensations are clear from the onset.

Another key aspect is to be mindful of the content you're publishing. Ensure that nothing you post can be construed as libel or defamation. It might be tempting to ride the waves of controversial content for quick gains, but the repercussions could sink your ship. Stay true to content that reflects positivity and provides value, and you'll find that your audience grows not only in number but in loyalty as well.

Handling financial transactions online requires the same caution. Whether it's incorporating your business for tax benefits or maintaining meticulous records, managing the fiscal aspect of your social media venture requires discipline and foresight. Using trusted payment processors and keeping abreast of changes in online commerce regulations will safeguard your profits.

Data protection should also be at the forefront of your operational procedures. As a custodian of your audience's data, whether it's their email addresses or payment information, you hold a responsibility to protect their privacy. Be transparent about your data use policies and stick to them religiously. Data breaches are not just financially damaging; they are trust shattering.

Don't overlook the importance of diversifying your income streams. By spreading your investments and revenue-generating activities across various platforms and mediums, you reduce the risk of seeing your income plummet should one platform suddenly change its algorithms or terms of service. Balance is key; focus on building multiple pillars to support your online business empire.

Moreover, staying educated about current and emerging online trends is another form of protection. What's permissible now might become a breach tomorrow. Keep your finger on the pulse of social media evolution—this proactive approach will arm you against being caught off-guard by new regulations or changes in platform policies.

When it comes to taxes, hiring an experienced tax professional who understands the intricacies of online income can save you from a world of financial pain. Don't let the complexity of tax laws deter you—seek expert advice to ensure you're not unnecessarily parting with your hard-earned money and are in compliance with the law.

Also, always have an exit strategy. Part of protecting yourself and your profits online is knowing when to pivot or call it quits. If a particular venture isn't yielding the desired outcomes despite your best efforts, it's wise to cut your losses and reallocate your resources into more fruitful endeavors.

A vital component often overlooked is insuring your business. Yes, even in the digital sphere, insurance plays a critical role. This could mean getting coverage for general liability to professional indemnity. Ensuring that you have proper protection in place for unforeseen circumstances is a hallmark of a savvy online entrepreneur.

Lastly, cultivate a support network of trusted advisors, mentors, and fellow creators. The digital landscape is not a solitary battlefield. By having a solid community around you, you receive not only moral support but also critical insights that can help you navigate the complexities of making money online safely and successfully.

In summary, making money through social media platforms is as much about creativity and engagement as it is about prudently safeguarding your and your audience's interests. By implementing the necessary protective measures, you are not erecting barriers but rather laying the foundation upon which a durable and prosperous online presence can be built. Keep these principles in mind, and your digital hustle will not only be rewarding but also remain robust in the face of ever-evolving online landscapes.

Chapter 12:
Beyond the Platforms:
Diversifying Your Online Income

Diving into the world of social media can often feel like navigating an ocean of endless opportunities. You've learnt the ropes of platforms like Facebook, Instagram, TikTok, and Threads, and perhaps you've started to see the fruits of your labor. But what happens when you want to push the envelope further? The secret to securing a resilient income stream online lies in diversification, and in this chapter, we're going to explore just how you can widen your horizons beyond the familiar online platforms.

Creating Your Own Products and Courses

Imagine transforming your knowledge and skills into a product that can be sold around the clock. Sounds enticing, right? It's not just a dream; it's a tangible reality for those willing to put in the effort. Whether it's an e-book detailing your social media strategies, an online course teaching photography for Instagram, or unique templates for social media posts, creating your own products means establishing an asset that works for you constantly.

The beauty of creating your own digital products is that it leverages your existing fan base and authority. You've worked hard to build trust, now it's time to capitalize on that by offering them even more value. Remember, the key is to understand the needs of your audience and develop products that solve their problems or enhance their skills.

Exploring Membership Sites and Patreon

Membership sites and platforms like Patreon shine a spotlight on the importance of community. They offer a method of monetizing your fan base by providing exclusive content, access, or experiences for a recurring fee. Think of this approach as developing a VIP club for your most devoted followers. They receive additional value, and you receive consistent, predictable income.

This form of revenue isn't just passive; it's also incredibly personal. You're not just selling a product; you're inviting your audience on a more intimate journey and rewarding their loyalty. Not only does this strengthen the bond with your audience, but it also provides financial stability to your online business that ad revenue and sponsorships may not always deliver.

Remember, diversifying your online income isn't just about the money. It's about building resilience into your digital empire, broadening your portfolio, and ensuring that you're not dependent on any single source of income. By creating products and cultivating a membership community, you are taking critical steps towards a future where your online presence is as sustainable as it is successful.

Creating Your Own Products and Courses

The landscape of online income is ever-changing, and platforms come and go. But one revenue stream that stands the test of time is creating your own products and courses. It's a method that provides control over your income and establishes you as an authority in your niche. Whether it's an ebook that dives deep into a specialized topic, or a full-fledged online course that shares your unique skills, these products can become the cornerstone of your digital empire.

Embarking on the product creation journey requires clarity and strategy. You've already built a reputation and a following on social media; now, it's time to leverage that audience by offering them something of tangible value. Think about the questions they ask you, the tips they seek from your content, and the problems they're looking to solve. This process brings to light the perfect opportunities for product development that truly resonate with your followers.

While some may shy away from creating their own products due to fears of complexity, this endeavor need not be daunting. Start small. A simple PDF guide or a short video series can act as your entry point into the world of digital products. With every step, test the waters to gauge your audience's interest and collect feedback that guides you in refining your product offerings.

Diving deeper into course creation, the e-learning market is booming, and there's a place for everyone willing to share knowledge. Platforms like Teachable, Udemy, and Skillshare have simplified the process, but creating courses on your own site gives you the ultimate control and profit margin. Your course can cover any topic you're passionate and knowledgeable about, from photography tips to financial literacy.

Keep in mind the importance of production quality. It doesn't require a Hollywood budget, but clear visuals and audio can make or break your course's success. Invest in a decent microphone, ensure good lighting, and plan your content meticulously. This professionalism elevates your brand and helps justify your pricing.

Pricing your products and courses is an art in itself. It involves understanding your audience's budget, assessing the value you're offering, and considering the competitive landscape. Don't sell yourself short, but also be realistic. It can be tempting to price high, but finding a balance that reinforces the worth of your expertise while remaining attainable to your audience is key.

Marketing is the bridge that connects your product to your potential customers. Use your social media presence as the primary channel for promotion. Tell a story about your product, why it's unique, how it can help, and the results it can bring. Utilize testimonials from early customers to add credibility and stir up excitement.

Email marketing complements social media perfectly. An email list gives you direct access to your audience in a space that's not controlled by an algorithm. It allows for a more personal approach, where you can nurture leads with free content before presenting your paid offer. Using this method creates a funnel that increases your conversion rates significantly.

Don't forget to leverage partnerships and affiliate marketing. By collaborating with other creators or influencers in your niche, you can tap into new audiences. Affiliates get a commission for sales generated through their referral, incentivizing them to promote your product more effectively than any ad campaign could.

Another key component is customer support. When someone invests in your product or course, they're investing in you. Therefore, providing top-notch customer service is not optional— it's an essential aspect of the product experience. Respond to inquiries promptly, resolve issues effectively, and ensure your customers feel valued.

Moreover, always collect and act on feedback. It's a goldmine that allows you to adjust your product for better performance, add new features, or address gaps you hadn't considered. This constant evolution keeps your product relevant and sustains sales over the long term.

If you're wondering about topics for your courses or products, reflect on your own experiences. How did you grow your social media? What skills have you acquired along the way? What knowledge do you possess that's in demand? The answers to these questions are often directly linked to viable product ideas.

Remember, passive income doesn't mean no work. It means doing a great deal of work upfront to reap rewards down the line. Your products and courses, once created, can be sold an infinite number of times without needing to start from scratch. It's a scalable way to build your income while focusing on creating more content, products, or even taking that well-deserved vacation.

Last but not least, stay adaptable and innovative. The online world changes rapidly, and what works today might not work tomorrow. Read the trends, listen to your audience, and be willing to iterate swiftly. It's this flexibility coupled with a solid product foundation that'll help you thrive beyond the platforms.

In the next chapter, we'll explore other avenues of income diversification. But let the idea of creating your own products and courses marinate. It's more than just a revenue stream; it's an extension of your brand and a testament to your expertise and creativity. Your journey to diversify your online income begins with the understanding that you're not just a content creator; you're an entrepreneur ready to shape your destiny.

Exploring Membership Sites and Patreon

When it comes to expanding your online income, one of the most engaging and rewarding strategies is through membership sites and Patreon. These platforms enable dedicated followers to become more than just passive spectators; they can actively participate in supporting your creative journey. With a membership model, you're inviting your audience into an exclusive circle, offering them unique content, special access, or perks in exchange for a recurring fee. It's a win-win situation: you gain a predictable stream of income, and your members receive added value that isn't available to just anyone.

Understanding the allure of this model is simple. As humans, we seek connection and exclusivity. We're drawn to closed communities and insider benefits. Membership sites and services like Patreon harness this desire, enabling you to create an intimate experience for your supporters. Think of it as a VIP club for your most dedicated fans—a place where they can gather, interact, and receive content that makes them feel valued.

To start, clarify what you can offer that's worth paying for. This must be something beyond what you already provide for free on social media. It could be in-depth tutorials, behind-the-scenes content, early access to your merchandise, or personalized advice. Listen to your audience; find out what they crave and tailor your offerings to meet those desires.

Patreon is a trailblazer in this space, providing a platform that's ubiquitous with the creator economy. It simplifies the process of setting up memberships by handling the technical aspects, payments, and subscriber management. This allows you to focus on what you do best—creating. With a variety of tiers, you can offer different levels of access or perks, each with its own price point, catering to various levels of engagement and financial commitment from your patrons.

However, leveraging membership sites or Patreon is not solely about the monetary gain. It's about nurturing a community and rewarding their loyalty. Engaging with your members, seeking their input, and making them feel heard is crucial. Your members are your allies, your brand ambassadors, and in many cases, your friends. You're not just building a revenue stream; you're cultivating relationships.

Take the time to communicate regularly with your members. Offer them exclusive updates and involve them in choices about your content creation—maybe through polls or discussions. This form of exclusive interaction cements their commitment to your brand and can lead to high retention rates.

Don't underestimate the importance of exclusivity in your content. People want to feel like they're getting something special. For instance, if you're known for your captivating travel blogs, consider creating member-only travel guides or share personal anecdotes and tips that you keep off your public channels. This exclusive content should not only be varied and rich but also consistent—you must deliver on your promises to retain subscribers.

Transparency is also crucial when running a membership site or using Patreon. Be upfront about where the money goes. Your patrons will appreciate knowing how their contributions help you and are likely to continue backing you when they see their support in action—whether it's funding new equipment, helping cover travel costs for that next great story, or simply allowing you to dedicate more time to content creation.

Marketing your membership program is another key area. Leverage your social media presence to introduce your audience to your membership options. Create enticing teasers that give them a taste of what they can expect. It's important to communicate the value of joining your membership. Highlight success stories or testimonials from current members that illustrate the benefits and foster a sense of community.

Pricing your tiers can be a balancing act. It's essential to find a price that reflects the value of your offering without being prohibitive. Start with a few tiers and refine as you go. The feedback you receive from your initial members can be priceless in adjusting your offerings.

Remember, building a stable income through membership programs takes time. You'll need to experiment, learn from your experiences, and evolve your strategy. Patience and persistence are key. Engage with your community, iterate on your content, and always look for fresh ways to add value for your members.

Membership sites and Patreon are excellent tools for diversifying your online income, but they also have the potential to transform your relationship with your audience. They're not just contributing financially; they're investing in your brand and in you as a creator. This commitment can be incredibly motivating, giving you the confirmation that there is a demand for your unique voice and content.

Lastly, it's important to stay informed and innovate. The online landscape is always changing. New platforms rise and old ones fall. Keep an eye on the horizon for fresh opportunities to engage your audience and grow your membership. Always strive to offer something that can't easily be replicated, and you'll find that your membership site or Patreon can become a cornerstone of your diversified online income.

In essence, think of membership sites and Patreon as a partnership between you and your most loyal followers. It's a powerful extension of your brand that if managed with care and creativity, opens doors to not just financial stability, but also a deeply engaged community that champions your success.

Conclusion

In the pages that have come before, we've journeyed through the expansive landscape of social media monetization. From Facebook to TikTok, Instagram to Threads, we've unveiled a myriad of strategies that can turn your online presence into a robust stream of income. As we draw this manual to a close, it's essential to distill the essence of sustaining your social media success into practical, enduring advice.

Sustaining Your Social Media Success

Your quest to make money from home isn't simply about getting started; it's about maintaining momentum and continually adapting to the ever-evolving dynamics of the digital world. The keys to longevity in this game hinge on a few core principles: staying informed, being adaptable, engaging authentically, and always bringing value to your audience.

You must keep abreast of trending topics, platform updates, and changes in algorithms. But more than that, you've got to be ready to pivot when a strategy doesn't pan out, or when a new opportunity presents itself. Remember, versatility isn't a luxury in this digital hustle—it's a necessity.

Engagement is a two-way street, and the relationships you build with your followers are the bedrock of your online enterprise. Your success is intertwined with your audience's loyalty and trust. Continue to hone your content to speak directly to their needs and desires, and you'll find strides in your growth and monetization efforts.

The online world is crowded and competitive, but there's always room at the top for genuine, innovative, and quality content. Ensuring that every post, video, or tweet you put out there adds value to someone's day will set you apart as a creator worth following—and worth buying from.

Lastly, remember that making money online is an exciting journey, not just a destination. There will be bumps along the way, perhaps even setbacks. But with each challenge, you'll gain invaluable insights that will fortify your resolve and your business acumen. Keep learning, stay flexible, and embrace your unique voice. Your potential, much like the realm of social media itself, is limitless.

Embark on this adventure with vision and determination. You're not just building an income; you're creating a legacy of content that resonates and inspires. And with that, let's wrap up this comprehensive guide, as you step forth to make your mark on the digital world!

Sustaining Your Social Media Success

You've made it to the conclusion of your journey, but remember that sustaining your success on social media is an ongoing process. It's a vibrant, ever-changing landscape where today's triumphs don't necessarily guarantee tomorrow's victories. Your ability to adapt and grow with the platform's changes will set you apart in the digital hustle.

The first key to lasting success is consistency. You can't simply post sporadically and expect your audience to remain engaged. Set up a content calendar and stick to it. Whether it's daily, thrice a week, or weekly posts, ensure that your followers have something to look forward to at regular intervals. This consistency fosters trust and keeps your audience invested in your brand.

Engagement is another cornerstone of sustained success. Social media is a two-way street; responding to comments, messages, and engaging with your audience's content makes them feel valued. It strengthens the relationship you have with your followers, which in turn increases loyalty and the likelihood that they'll recommend your brand to others.

Be ready to evolve as well. What works today may not work tomorrow. Staying abreast of trends and platform updates is crucial. Always be willing to learn, whether it's a new feature on Instagram or a fresh way to monetize content on TikTok. Keeping a finger on the pulse of social media ensures that you're never left behind.

Quality of content should never take a backseat. As the saying goes, content is king. Investing time in producing high-quality, compelling, and shareable content will always pay off. Remember, it's not just about the quantity—you must deliver value with each post.

Analysis is a powerful tool for sustainability. Regularly analyze your performance using platform analytics tools and adjust your strategy accordingly. If certain types of posts garner more engagement or shares, consider producing more content in that vein. Don't be afraid to drop what isn't working.

Remember to remain authentic. As you grow, it may be tempting to cut corners or change your messaging to cater to broader audiences. However, authenticity is key to your brand's identity. Your followers are savvy—they can sense when content isn't genuine, which can lead to a loss of trust.

Networking shouldn't stop. Continue to collaborate with influencers and brands that align with your values. These partnerships can extend your reach, bring fresh perspectives to your content, and provide additional revenue streams.

Always stay legally compliant. As you monetize your presence, ensure you're adhering to all the necessary disclosures, copyright laws, and sponsorship agreements. The legal aspect of social media is not just a formality; it protects your content, reputation, and profits.

Diversify your income sources. Don't put all your eggs in one basket. Use your social media success as a springboard to explore other income-generating ventures, such as creating e-courses, merchandise, or even writing a book. Multiple revenue streams ensure you're not overly reliant on one platform or source of income.

Keep learning and upskilling. The social media realm constantly introduces new tools and technologies that can enhance content creation and distribution. Invest in courses, attend webinars, and practice using new tools to remain competitive and improve efficiency.

Self-care is incredibly important. Avoid burnout by taking regular breaks and managing your workload effectively. Remember, you can always use tools to automate some of your processes, giving you more time to recharge and maintain that creative edge.

In times when you feel overwhelmed, it takes courage to ask for help. Whether it's hiring a freelancer, using a virtual assistant, or simply reaching out to a peer for advice, don't shoulder all the burden alone. Outsourcing can free up your time and introduce new skills and ideas to your strategy.

Lastly, celebrate your successes, no matter how small. Every new follower, every successful post, and every milestone is a testament to your hard work. These celebrations keep the journey enjoyable and motivating, propelling you to strive for more.

To wrap it up, sustaining your social media success is a continuous effort made up of learning, evolving, and staying committed to your values and vision. It's about creating balance while seizing opportunities to innovate and grow. Your path to success doesn't end here—it only gets more exciting as you build upon the solid foundation you've established.

Appendix A: Appendix

You've journeyed through the digital landscape, uncovering the vast opportunities for making money right from your fingertips. Now, as you stand poised and ready to pivot from theory to action, harness the full potential of social media with this comprehensive resource directory. It's your go-to guide for the tools, platforms, and services that will catapult you into social media monetization success.

Resource Directory: Tools, Platforms, and Services

In a realm teeming with resources, it can be daunting to pinpoint exactly what you need to thrive online. But fret not; we've curated a robust list tailored for your ascent in the social media stratosphere. Below, find an overview of platforms and tools crucial to your endeavor. We cover a spectrum that spans content creation, analytics, content management, and networking – essential components in your social media wealth toolkit.

- **Content Creation:**

Unleash your creative prowess with applications and software designed for high-quality content. These include editing apps for videos and images that ensure your visuals are cutting-edge and engaging.

- **Analytics:**

Use these platforms to glean insights about your audience, track your growth, and fine-tune your strategy. Detailed analytics tools will help you understand what works and what doesn't, allowing you to focus on high-impact activities.

- **Scheduling and Automation:**

Efficiency is key to managing your social media presence. Discover tools that allow you to schedule posts in advance, automate engagement, and streamline your workflow, freeing up more time to craft your next viral masterpiece.

- **Networking and Outreach:**

Building a network is non-negotiable in the online world. Leverage platforms that enable you to connect with brands, fellow influencers, and potential collaborators who can amplify your reach and resources.

Remember, the tools and services outlined here should be seen as mechanisms to propel you forward. They will refine and enhance the strategies you've learned, but your unique flair, creativity, and commitment will remain the heartbeat of your online enterprise.

As you pore over this appendix, remember that the technology landscape is ever-evolving. Keep an eye out for emerging tools that can give you an edge, and don't be afraid to experiment. Find what meshes seamlessly with your personal brand and audience.

Embrace the myriad of resources at your disposal. They're not merely a means to an end, but partners on this thrilling journey. Empower yourself with knowledge, equip yourself with the right tools, and carve a path to digital prosperity that is uniquely yours.

It's your time to shine online.

Resource Directory: Tools, Platforms, and Services

As you embark on this journey of making money through social media, it's invaluable to have a go-to list of resources at your disposal. This directory is designed to help you navigate the plethora of tools, platforms, and services that will support your quest for online income. Whether you're a beginner or a seasoned content creator, these resources are foundational elements in your toolkit.

Let's start with the platforms that serve as your virtual stage. You're already familiar with Facebook, Instagram, TikTok, and Threads. These social media giants are pivotal in your strategy, but there are also other platforms worth your attention, such as YouTube for video content, Pinterest for image curation, and Twitch or Mixer for live streaming, considering your niche and audience preferences.

Next, for content creation and management, tools like Canva and Adobe Spark simplify graphic design, even for those with limited experience. They offer easy-to-use templates and a user-friendly interface that can help you produce eye-catching imagery that complements your posts and videos.

When it comes to video editing, platforms like Final Cut Pro and Adobe Premiere Pro are industry standards for a reason—they pack powerful editing capabilities that can elevate your video content. But for simpler alterations, tools like InShot or FilmoraGo offer sufficient functionality right from your phone.

To maintain a consistent and impactful presence, social media scheduling tools like Buffer, Hootsuite, or Later become necessary. They allow you to plan and automate your posts, so you never miss the opportunity to engage with your audience or promote your content at optimal times.

For those who are looking to tap into the analytics side of social media, consider using platforms like Google Analytics for tracking website traffic, and social platform-specific insights tools to comprehend audience behavior, which will inform your strategy and content creation.

Monetizing your audience requires connecting with the right brands and opportunities. Influencer marketplaces such as AspireIQ, Upfluence, and BrandSnob can streamline the process of finding sponsorship and partnership opportunities that align with your brand.

As you grow, email marketing remains a potent tool to directly reach your followers. Services like Mailchimp and ConvertKit offer robust systems to manage your email lists and campaigns, allowing for personalized communication and deeper connections with your audience.

If you're venturing into ecommerce, integrating Shopify or WooCommerce with your social media can create seamless shopping experiences for your followers. These platforms provide comprehensive solutions to manage your online store and integrate with your social accounts.

For creators leaning towards live interactions, webinar and live workshop platforms such as Zoom and Google Meet enable you to connect with your audience in real-time, which can be monetized through premium access, memberships or exclusive content.

Those planning on offering courses or educational content can look to platforms like Teachable, Udemy, or Skillshare, where you can create and sell your courses to eager learners worldwide. They provide the infrastructure to support your teaching endeavors.

If outsourcing content creation or other tasks becomes a necessity, freelancing platforms such as Fiverr and Upwork can connect you with professionals who can take your ideas and execute them effectively. They're excellent for finding writers, graphic designers, video editors, and more.

Finally, protecting your creations and understanding your rights is crucial. Consider using copyright services like Copyright.com or Creative Commons to secure your work, and enlist legal services such as LegalZoom or your local attorney for advice on contracts and agreements with brands.

Always remember, the success of your social media journey is significantly influenced by the tools and services you utilize. By choosing the right combination that fits your workflow, your brand, and your audience, you can streamline your operations and focus more on creating content that resonates and drives income.

This directory isn't exhaustive but serves as a solid foundation from which to launch. Keep an eye out for emerging tools and platforms, as the digital landscape is always evolving. Staying ahead of the curve is key to maintaining and cultivating a lucrative online presence. Now dive in, explore these resources, and let them catapult you towards achieving your social media financial goals.

Glossary of Social Media Terms

Transitioning from the plethora of strategies and insights, let's streamline your journey with a definitive glossary of social media terms. This clarity will serve as your compass, navigating you through the ever-evolving lexicon of the digital landscape, ensuring that not a single tweet, post, or viral moment throws you off course.

Algorithm

An algorithm is a complex set of instructions that social media platforms use to determine which content is displayed to users, when it's displayed, and to whom. Understanding these can give you a strategic edge in placing your content in front of the right eyes at the right time.

Analytics

Analytics provide invaluable data about your social media performance. These insights, ranging from engagement rates to audience demographics, can inform your content strategy and ultimately, your potential earnings.

Brand Ambassador

A brand ambassador is someone who partners with companies to promote products or services. Inherent credibility and trust with an audience make this role a lucrative one if you can secure it.

Content Calendar

This is a schedule of when and what you'll post on social media. A well-planned content calendar is a key to maintaining a consistent presence and keeping your audience engaged.

Engagement Rate

Engagement rate is a metric for assessing interactions with your content such as likes, comments, and shares. Higher engagement rates can lead to increased visibility and opportunities to monetize.

Followers

Followers are individuals who subscribe to receive your updates on social media platforms. The size and interaction of your follower base can have a direct impact on your online income potential.

Hashtag

A hashtag is a keyword or phrase preceded by the pound sign (#) and used to categorize content. Effective use of hashtags can catapult your content into larger conversations and reach wider audiences.

Influencer

An influencer is a social media user who has established credibility within a specific industry, has access to a large audience, and can persuade others by virtue of their authenticity and reach. Influencers can monetize their influence through brand partnerships, sponsorships, and more.

Monetization

Monetization is turning your social media activities into revenue streams. This could include sponsored posts, affiliate marketing, selling products, or other creative revenue-generating tactics.

Sponsored Post

A sponsored post is content that a user creates to promote a brand or product, for which they're compensated. Full transparency is key to maintaining trust with your audience when creating sponsored content.

Stories

Stories are temporary posts that appear for only 24 hours on platforms like Instagram and Facebook. They're a fantastic way to engage with your audience in a more casual, fleeting way. Don't underestimate their power for promotion and connection.

User-Generated Content (UGC)

UGC is content created by unpaid contributors or fans which can range from images to videos and reviews. Brands often share UGC to build community and authenticity, and creators can leverage this for exposure and credibility.

Employ each term with precision, and you'll articulate your strategies and engage your audience with the expertise of a seasoned social media maestro. Ride the wave of the digital economy's potential and let these terms guide you to the shores of success.

Frequently Asked Questions: Quick Answers to Common Concerns

In the following section, we dive into the FAQs - those burning questions that most social media aspirants grapple with on their journey to digital prosperity.

Frequently Asked Questions: Quick Answers to Common Concerns

Social media can seem like a maze with too many turns and twists, especially if you're keen on turning those likes, follows, and shares into dollar signs. Questions abound, and here, you'll get crisp, clear answers to some of the most common queries that might be stewing in your entrepreneurial mind.

How do I pick the right platform to make money on?

Think about where your strengths lie and which format best showcases your content. Are you more comfortable with photos and visuals? Instagram might be your stage. If you're into crafting engaging stories in under a minute, TikTok calls out to you. For dialogue and community building, consider Facebook. Remember, engagement and content value beat the platform's popularity – it's where your content thrives that counts!

Can I really earn money from short video content?

Absolutely! TikTok and similar short-video platforms have made it possible for creators to monetize their content through brand deals, live gifts, and even TikTok's Creator Fund once you hit their criteria. The key is to create content that resonates and engages - the more you grip your audience, the more opportunities will come knocking.

What's the making of a powerful social media presence?

Authenticity, consistency, and engagement. Understand your unique value and share it with the world regularly. Interact with your followers and build a community. Be the voice they trust, and you'll have not just an audience, but a fanbase ready to support your monetization efforts.

Are followers the same as dollars?

Not directly, but they are potential dollars. A large follower count opens doors to sponsorships and partnerships, but what really matters is engagement. An engaged audience is more likely to answer your call-to-actions, purchase your products, or hit those affiliate links.

Do I need to be viral to earn from social media?

Not at all. Virality can be a flash in the pan. Sure, it helps to gain exposure, but consistent, value-driven content ensures a steady income stream. Think of virality as a bonus, not the business plan.

How important is understanding social media algorithms?

Knowing how the algorithms work can be a game-changer. They dictate who sees your content and when. Ride the algorithmic wave by timing your posts right and using popular hashtags to increase your visibility and the chance of hitting it big.

Can I manage everything on my own, or should I outsource?

Both strategies have merits. DIY keeps you in control and intimate with your content and audience. Outsourcing, on the other hand, can free up your time for strategy and new content creation. Evaluate your strengths and time management to make the choice that best serves your goals.

What type of content sells best?

Content that sells is content that solves a problem, entertains, or informs. It must resonate with your audience's needs and desires. Understand your niche, and tailor your content to stand out. That's the golden ticket.

Is it sustainable to make social media my primary source of income?

It can be, but diversification is key. Don't put all your eggs in one social media basket. Explore creating your own products, affiliate marketing, memberships, and more. The more streams of income, the merrier your wallet.

Should I focus on just one social media platform?

It's wise to start with one and master it before stretching too thin. Once you have a good grip, branching out can help you expand your reach and secure your income against the volatile nature of social media trends.

Are there legal concerns I should be aware of?

Yes, understanding the legalities of copyright, sponsorships, and disclosures is crucial. These protect you and your reputation. Be transparent with your audience about sponsored content, and respect intellectual property to steer clear of legal headaches.

How do I craft perfect video content?

Focus on the value you're providing. Videos should be clear, engaging, and edited for a smooth viewing experience. It's less about perfection and more about connection and truthfulness in conveying your message.

What's the most efficient way to grow my social media presence?

Engage with your audience, collaborate with others in your niche, and use social media tools for analytics and scheduling. Keep learning and adapting. Social media is ever-changing, so stay open and agile.

Can I use social media to sell my own products?

Of course! Social media offers a prime arena to showcase your products. Use your channels to tell your product's story, demonstrate its value, and connect with customers. It's about making genuine connections that lead to sales.

How frequently should I post content?

Consistency is more important than frequency. Find a rhythm that keeps your audience engaged without burning you out. Use insights and analytics to determine when your audience is most active, and tailor your schedule to that sweet spot.

www.ingramcontent.com/pod-product-compliance
Lightning Source LLC
Chambersburg PA
CBHW022000170526
45157CB00003B/1080